An Album of

Hull & Barnsley Railway Engines and Rolling Stock 1885

Martin Barker

CONTENTS

INTRODUCTION

This book is a photographic record of the original rolling stock of the Hull, Barnsley and West Riding Junction Railway and Dock Company, or as it was popularly known (and officially so after 1905), the Hull and Barnsley Railway. They were taken on behalf of the rolling stock builders to provide accurate records of examples of each type of vehicle immediately before entering service.

The designer of the stock was William Kirtley, locomotive Superintendent of the London, Chatham and Dover Railway - seemingly an unlikely choice by the H&BR's Directors. He was engaged temporarily as Consulting Engineer on the recommendation of James Staats Forbes, Chairman and Managing Director of the LC&DR, and an influential member of the H&BR Board. Kirtley was well established: in February (the time of his engagement by the H&BR). 54 engines to his designs were working on the LC&DR, with others on order or under construction. He had served an apprenticeship under his uncle Matthew Kirtley at the Midland Railway's Derby Works continuing to make a career with that Company, until his LC&DR appointment in 1874. He retired in 1899 upon the amalgamation of the LC&DR with its rival the South Eastern Railway to form the South Eastern and Chatham Railway. Kirtley's locomotives proved more effective than those by James Stirling, Locomotive Superintendent of the bigger South Eastern Railway - South Eastern & Chatham locomotives up to 1914 perpetuated many Kirtley features.

Rather ironically, Stirling family honour was upheld on the H&BR, with the permanent appointment as Locomotive Superintendent of James Stirling's nephew, Matthew. Born in 1856, two years after William Kirtley began his apprenticeship, Matthew Stirling's relative youthfulness did not prevent him from slight criticism of his predecessor's work, and with some justification as we shall see. Suffice to say that when locomotives to Matthew Stirling's first design appeared in 1889, they were appreciably more powerful than Kirtley's Class B and differed considerably in appearance, Stirling having drawn on his Doncaster training under his father Patrick, for inspiration.

From being appointed H&BR Consultant on 19th February 1883, Kirtley produced drawings and specifications of the locomotives for the Board's approval on 30th March. A mere 35 or so working days would be nowhere near enough time to have drawn out three detailed designs single-handed (as well as keeping on top of his department on the LC&DR). So Kirtley either used existing detail drawings of fittings from Chatham engines, or more probably the detail designing was part of the work tendered out. In any case, Kirtley most likely presented the H&BR Board with simple outline diagrams and specifications. Only James Staats Forbes had any locomotive engineering experience and to the untrained eye, fully-detailed, sectional locomotive drawings can appear fearsomely complex; so no Board member would proffer any doubts.

The H&BR Board's next step was to determine passenger and goods vehicle requirements. This was done somewhat empirically by studying numbers of carriages and wagons per mile on other railways and again William Kirtley was invited to submit passenger and goods rolling stock designs, which he did on 22nd June 1883. This time the Board deliberated longer than for the locomotives since it was 20th July before he was authorised to invite the first tenders, for 34 carriages. Further tenders were accepted on 11th January 1884, and 55 more vehicles were ordered on 26th February. The same day also saw Kirtley authorised to draw up specifications for a breakdown train.

The first locomotives were delivered in 1884 and by the end of June 1885 39 items of carriage stock had also been delivered, in good time for the line's opening on 27th July. By the end of the year all the initial orders had been completed.

Taking the most charitable view, the carriages, all four-wheeled, were decidedly antiquated even for 1885 but it was hardly surprising that William Kirtley should provide archaic carriages. Neither the London, Chatham & Dover Railway nor the South Eastern Railway were renowned for sumptuous accommodation - rather the opposite. With the exception of stock built for boat train workings and the like, both companies' more usual items of stock were thirty or forty years behind the times. So what was good enough for the London commuter or Kentish hop-picker was obviously good enough for the North Country businessman, West Riding miner or Hull docker, at least as far as Kirtley was concerned.

2nd October 1905 saw a through Hull to Sheffield Midland service start, thanks to the Midland Railway granting running powers to the H&BR from its western terminus at Cudworth near Barnsley, over Midland metals to Sheffield. They even lent the H&BR a number of their six-wheeled carriages but required their return by 30th April 1906. Meanwhile modern bogie coaches were on order by the H&BR, but sadly delivery of these was delayed until February 1907. One can only feel sympathy for the H&BR Board, embarrassed and humiliated by having to employ their antediluvian four-wheelers on their new through service. Luckily the Midland Railway's crimson-lake carriages were too distinctively different for their patrons to run any risk of confusing them with the H&BR's more modest conveyances.

Little need be written here regarding the goods vehicles, the first orders were fulfilled in 1885 for 530 vehicles. The H&BR's rolling stock Committee of 1883 had projected a total requirement of 1,300 wagons, a target reached in the mid-1890's although deliveries of wagons tended to be to Matthew Stirling's specifications, rather than those of William Kirtley. True to form Kirtley provided near copies of existing London, Chatham & Dover designs and of all his work for the H&BR the wagons lasted longer in main line service than the locomotives or carriages.

ACKNOWLEDGEMENTS

In the preparation of this work I am very grateful for drawings provided by Nick Fleetwood and the Late John C. Wright. Other members of the Hull and Barnsley Stock Fund have provided valuable encouragement and support, particularly Brian Crowther. I have also to thank the custodians of the North Eastern Railway Association Library and the Ken Hoole Study Centre, Darlington Railway Museum, for the provision of extra illustrative material. I would also like to thank Mick Nicholson and Peter Devine for help on this script.

Plate 1 **H&BR Class A 0-6-0 Tank Locomotive, No. 12.** Taken in photograph grey livery before delivery from Beyer Peacock in 1885 (works No. 2614). These engines later became Class G1.

4

CLASS A 0-6-0 TANK LOCOMOTIVES, Nos. 1 - 12

After the H&BR board sanctioned Kirtley to invite tenders, that submitted by Beyer, Peacock & Co., of Manchester was accepted and the contract signed on 24th April 1883. Each locomotive was steam–braked only, but it was decided to fit Nos. 1-6 with Westinghouse air brakes, which increased their costs by £89 each above the price of £2,170 for the unfitted locomotives. Their builder's numbers were 2430-4, 2436-41, and 2614; six were to be delivered in May 1884 and the rest in June. Some however, were delivered early in 1885 and No. 12 appeared late in 1885 - after all the Class B and C locomotives had been built, if its works number is used as an indicator. No. 2435 was diverted by the builders to the Rhondda & Swansea Bay Railway; they had ordered a shunting locomotive and the H&BR had just run out of money, hence doubts about payments had arisen. The Class A were very similar to the existing Class T of the London, Chatham and Dover Railway of which two examples only had appeared in December 1879. The H&BR locomotives were an improvement on their two 'cousins' since their coal bunker capacity was increased by $1/2$ ton to $1 1/4$ tons – a figure Kirtley used for eight more LC&DR engines which were built in 1889. The H&BR locomotives were slightly heavier due to having boilers of 4ft 3in diameter, 2in more than the LC&DR engines. The most noticeable difference between the two railways' classes was the shape of the cab cut–outs: the doors being symmetrically placed on the Class A but set further back on the LC&DR Class T.

Otherwise, most dimensions were identical - wheels were nominally 4ft 6in diameter, set at 7ft 4in and 7ft 8in centres (15ft overall), cylinders had a diameter of 17in and 24in stroke - all these were common to both classes. It may be worth pointing out that due to tyre wear or renewal, wheel diameters could vary by as much as 3in and that cylinder diameters could increase by as much as $1 1/2$ in by reboring to correct wear - which would alter horsepower figures in turn. Similarly, reboilering may affect weight, boiler pressure and consequently horse-power). As built, the Class A worked at 140 lb/in^2 boiler pressure, which taken at 85% in the cylinders gave a tractive effort of 15,284 lbs. Their nominal weight in working order was $42 1/4$ tons. Each side-tank held 850 gallons of water; the grate area (at 15 ft^2 represented 1/69th of the total boiler heating surface area. The boilers were of 7/16in Yorkshire Iron plates with copper inner fireboxes, stays and tubes, of which there were 199 at $1 3/4$ in outside diameter, pitched at $2 1/2$ in centres in horizontal rows.

A possible weakness was in the radius of the inner firebox side plates where they were bent inwards to join the top (crownsheet) plate. This was a mere $2 1/2$ in radius - "...too square a head" as Matthew Stirling put it, going on to state 6in as a more usual radius. (Too small a radius was liable to suffer cracking caused by expansion and contraction stresses set up in the boiler by heating and cooling)

The first locomotives delivered were set to work assisting in the construction of the railway but after the H&BR's opening they spent most of their mundane lives on shunting duties, being almost entirely based at Alexandra Dock Shed in Hull working for 12-14 hours per day - the contents of a bunkerful of coal. However, before the railway opened it was found that a 15ft wheelbase was too long for some of the tighter dockyard curves so six small, four-wheeled, well-tank locomotives of a standard design were ordered from Kitson & Co. of Leeds - only three of which were at work by the end of November 1887.

The Class A were relatively unchanged throughout their lives, retaining their domed boilers but eventually gaining Stirling's style of smokebox doors and chimneys and coal rails around the bunker tops, increasing the coal capacity. Stirling altered their appearance by slight changes to the colour scheme and made their identities more clear - the initials 'H & B R' appeared on the sidetanks. The number plates were moved to the bunker sides and

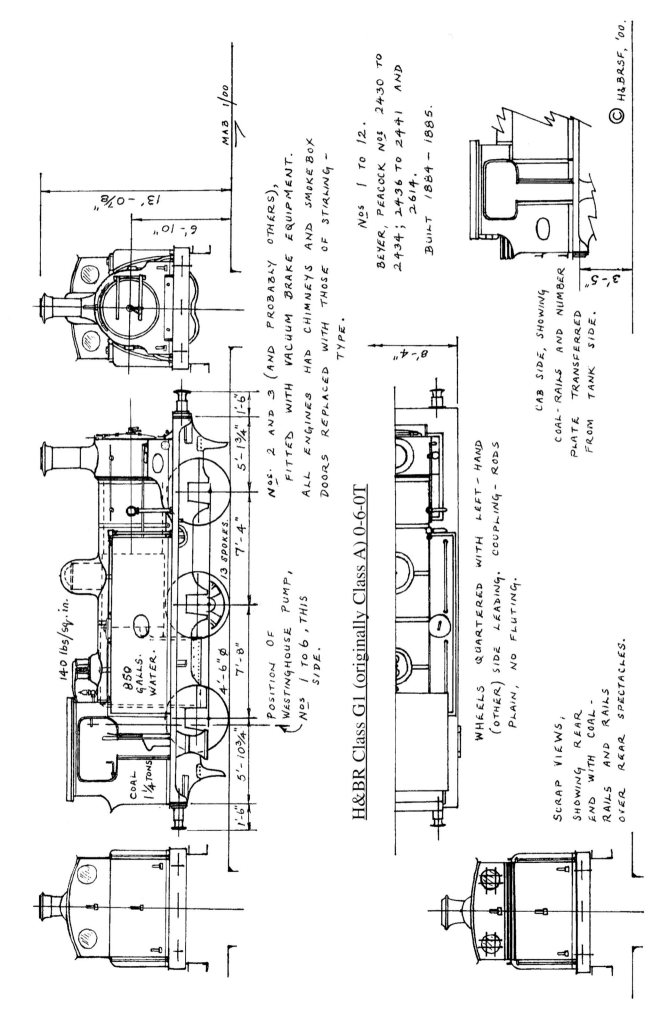

14.0 lbs/sq.in.

13'-0⅞"

6'-10"

5'-1¾" 1'-6"

7'-4"

13 SPOKES.

4'-6" Ø

7'-8"

850 GALLS. WATER.

COAL 1¼ TONS.

1'-6" 5'-10¾"

MAB 1/00

POSITION OF WESTINGHOUSE PUMP, Nos 1 TO 6, THIS SIDE.

Nos. 2 AND 3 (AND PROBABLY OTHERS), FITTED WITH VACUUM BRAKE EQUIPMENT. ALL ENGINES HAD CHIMNEYS AND SMOKE-BOX DOORS REPLACED WITH THOSE OF STIRLING TYPE.

Nos 1 TO 12. BEYER, PEACOCK Nos 2430 TO 2434; 2436 TO 2441 AND 2614. BUILT 1884-1885.

© H&BRSF, '00.

3'-5"

CAB SIDE, SHOWING COAL-RAILS AND NUMBER PLATE TRANSFERRED FROM TANK SIDE.

H&BR Class G1 (originally Class A) 0-6-0T

8'-4"

WHEELS QUARTERED WITH LEFT-HAND (OTHER) SIDE LEADING. COUPLING-RODS PLAIN, NO FLUTING.

SCRAP VIEWS; SHOWING REAR END WITH COAL-RAILS AND RAILS OVER REAR SPECTACLES.

Beyer, Peacock's plates in turn becoming bolted to the sandbox / splasher sides, above the leading wheels. The air-braked engines lost that equipment in the 1890's, and finally the entire class was redesignated as G1 in 1908.

With the North Eastern Railway absorption of the H&BR in 1922 as a prelude to the much larger Grouping of the following year the entire class was withdrawn; seven, including No. 12, were scrapped at Springhead Works, in Hull. However, Nos. 2-5, and No. 8 were resold for industrial use early in 1923. All went to the Ashington Coal Company except for No.5 which was bought by the Co-operative colliery at Shilbottle, calling in at Hawthorn, Leslie & Co. at Newcastle for overhaul en route to its new home.

The Ashington engines acquired various odd modifications - No. 4 as Ashington No. 19 received a very 'homemade' looking chimney at some time in its career and at least one of the others received an enlarged bunker (Nos. 2, 3, and 8 became Ashington 16, 17 and 18). In passing, it is worth mentioning that the last of the 'Chatham' soldiered on in main line service until British Railways withdrew it in July 1951. Two others had been sold for colliery shunting use: one on Tyneside and the other (the first of the Kirtley six-coupled tank locomotives dating from 1879) went to work at Haydock Colliery in Lancashire, remaining at work until September 1958 having outlived its H&BR. relatives at Ashington, the last of which had been withdrawn by July 1939.

Both types enjoyed long lives due to the excellence of the materials specified for their construction and the moderate boiler pressure, and had been popular with their crews. The writer can testify that at Ashington some thirty years after their demise, the verdict on the performance of Kirtley's H&BR tanks in comparison with a wide variety of other types was, "They were the best".

Further testimony lay in the fact that the Rhondda and Swansea Bay ordered further examples of Kirtley's H&BR design from Beyer, Peacock; all became Great Western Railway property, survived at work into the 1930's.

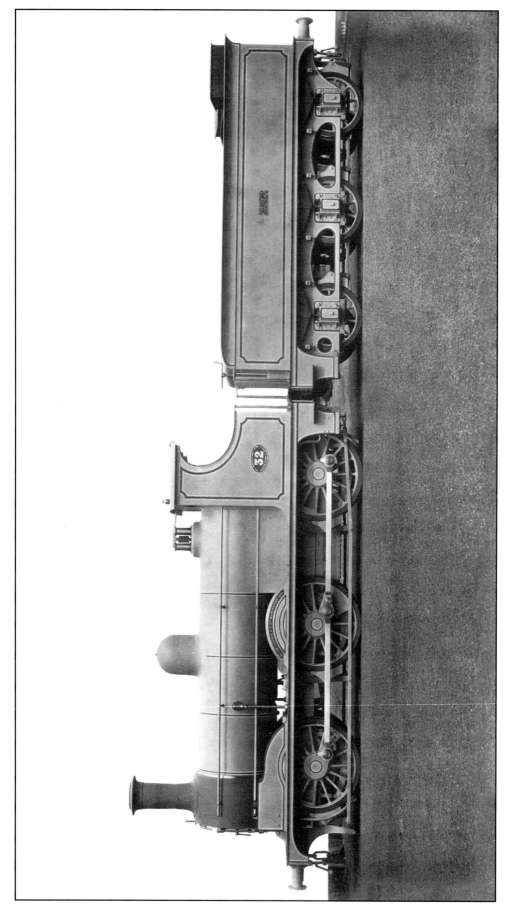

Plate 2 **H&BR Class B 0-6-0 Tender Locomotive, No. 32.** Beyer Peacock works No. 2508. No. 32 received a new domeless boiler and Stirling cab in the early 1900's becoming a member of the class D.

CLASS B 0-6-0 TENDER LOCOMOTIVES, Nos. 13 - 32

These twenty engines were provided for the H&BR to earn its bread and butter: hauling export coal from West Yorkshire. Derived from existing London, Chatham & Dover Railway types, they bore a striking visual resemblance to Kirtley's LC&DR B1 Class, but had more in common dimensionally with an 1861 design by his predecessor. Martley: the "Acis" (or H Class, under Kirtley's LC&DR classification system).

These latter and the H&BR 0-6-0's had 5ft diameter coupled wheels and 17ins x 24ins cylinders. Kirtley had completed work in reboilering the H's in 1881 so possibly he used the same boiler for the H&BR design, since common dimensions were diameters at 4ft 3ins, grate areas at 16.25ft^2 and boiler tubes – 199 at 1^3/$_4$ in diameter. Locomotive weights were virtually the same, at nearly 36 tons apiece.

Doubtless the H&BR 0-6-0's could have filled a satisfactory niche on the LC&DR; retrospectively it was a pity (for the H&BR), that their engines couldn't have been exchanged for their Kirtley predecessors of 1876 – the LC&DR's B1 Class. These, with easier work to do, had bigger cylinders and smaller wheels giving them a higher tractive effort; and with a slightly bigger grate area plus 50ft extra heating surface had the edge over the B's for making water boil.

The H&BR tenders had 3ft 9in diameter wheels at 6ft spacings, held 3^1/$_2$ tons of coal and 2,000 gallons of water.

Again, Beyer, Peacock built all the Class B's (works numbers 2489-2508), in 1885. Each cost £2,695, but Nos. 23-28 were £50 extra each, being fitted with Westinghouse brakes. No. 14 had the honour of working the H&BR's first passenger train, an inspection special for Company officers and guests on 28th May 1885, some two months before the line opened. Despite being brand new, No. 14 was overcome by the great occasion for it broke down at South Cave, causing two of the Contractor's small tank engines to be pressed into service.

Since no passenger engines were delivered until some three weeks after the H&BR opened, the 0-6-0's were responsible for all the main line traffic. Initially only three Westinghouse fitted engines were available, an insufficient number for covering all the passenger workings, but since legislation prohibiting the running of non-continuously braked passenger trains did not appear until 1889 it is probable that some workings relied on the locomotive steam brake and guard's handbrake in order to stop.

In a lecture in Hull given in 1887, Matthew Stirling gave some interesting statistics regarding the workings of the Class B's. Average goods train weights (including the locomotive, tender and 22 loaded wagons), were 284 tons, which the 0-6-0's were moving at an average 25 mph, consuming an average of 787^1/$_2$ lbs of coal per hour (each square foot of grate surface burning 48^1/$_2$ lbs per hour). This worked out at 31^1/$_2$ lbs of coal consumed per mile. From this we can work out that a tenderful of coal would take an H&BR train some 250 miles, assuming that the tender was topped up before moving "off shed" after raising steam. Not so evident though is that 31^1/$_2$ lbs per mile was a fairly high figure for a moderately sized locomotive, but crews had to be somewhat forceful in order to get the necessary work out of them. An indication of this was that at the same talk, Stirling remarked that some locomotive chimneys had already been replaced with tougher cast iron ones; the built-up Kirtley chimneys had centre sections made of Best Staffordshire Iron plate which had become eroded by severe cinder–cutting.

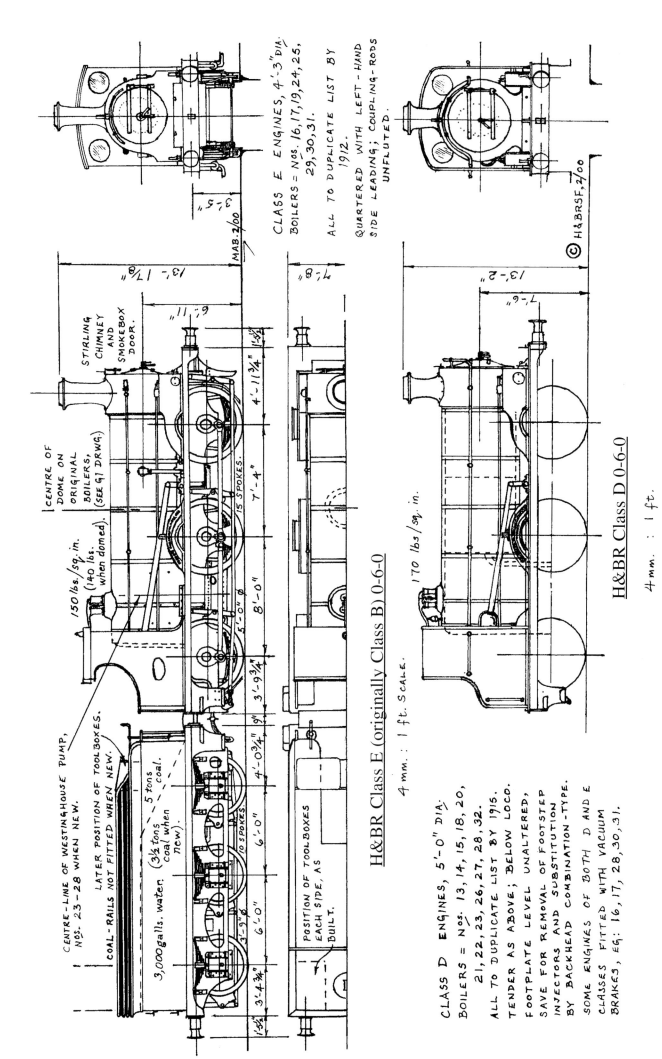

CLASS E ENGINES, 4'-3" DIA.
BOILERS = Nos. 16, 17, 19, 24, 25, 29, 30, 31.
ALL TO DUPLICATE LIST BY 1912.
QUARTERED WITH LEFT-HAND SIDE LEADING; COUPLING-RODS UNFLUTED.

MAB. 2/00

© H&BRSF, 2/00

STIRLING CHIMNEY AND SMOKEBOX DOOR.

CENTRE OF DOME ON ORIGINAL BOILERS, (SEE G1 DRWG.)

150 lbs/sq. in. (140 lbs. when domed).

COAL-RAILS NOT FITTED WHEN NEW.

CENTRE-LINE OF WESTINGHOUSE PUMP, Nos. 23-28 WHEN NEW.

LATER POSITION OF TOOLBOXES.

3,000 galls. water. (3½ tons coal when new).

5 tons coal.

POSITION OF TOOLBOXES EACH SIDE, AS BUILT.

H&BR Class E (originally Class B) 0-6-0

4 mm. : 1 ft. SCALE.

170 lbs/sq. in.

H&BR Class D 0-6-0

4 mm. : 1 ft.

CLASS D ENGINES, 5'-0" DIA.
BOILERS = Nos. 13, 14, 15, 18, 20, 21, 22, 23, 26, 27, 28, 32.
ALL TO DUPLICATE LIST BY 1915.
TENDER AS ABOVE; BELOW LOCO.
FOOTPLATE LEVEL UNALTERED, SAVE FOR REMOVAL OF FOOTSTEP INJECTORS AND SUBSTITUTION BY BACKHEAD COMBINATION-TYPE.
SOME ENGINES OF BOTH D AND E CLASSES FITTED WITH VACUUM BRAKES, EG: 16, 17, 28, 30, 31.

By 1897 Stirling began replacing boilers after twelve years of hard work, not only were chimneys wearing out. Initially boilers of the same diameter were fitted, but of characteristic Stirling domeless type. From 1902 domeless boilers 5ft diameter were fitted, necessitating new cabs of the Stirling short roofed style, the cast brass numberplates being replaced by transfers. Simultaneously with reboilering, cylinders were bored out to $17\frac{1}{2}$in diameter which, with a boiler pressure 10lb/in^2 higher and a slightly larger grate area, marginally improved the locomotives' abilities to master their work. The final locomotive/boiler outcome was:

4ft 3in diameter - Nos. 16, 17, 19, 24, 25, 29-31   : 1908 Class E
5ft 0in diameter - Nos. 13-15, 18, 20-23, 26-28,32   : 1908 Class D

1892 saw the H&BR change from Westinghouse to vacuum brakes; how this affected Nos. 23 to 28 is not known, although it would have made operational sense to have retained air brakes on some engines. Engines acquiring vacuum brakes included Nos. 16, 17, 28, 30 and 31. Probably around this time too the toolboxes were removed from the rear tender tank tops to the front end, being placed crossways to form some rearward protection for the crews, and three coal rails were also fitted aground the sides and ends.

From 1911 it was obvious the Class D and E were living on borrowed time: newly delivered Stirling Class L1 0-6-0's took Nos. 16, 17, 19, 24, 25, 29-32, causing the existing engines so numbered to be put on a duplicate list since the Company couldn't afford to scrap them immediately (Locomotives on the duplicate list received the letter 'A' painted on their cabsides). 1913 saw five Stirling Class F3 0-6-2 tank locomotives delivered, displacing Nos. 13, 15, 18, 23 and 27. Finally, more 0-6-0's (the five superheated LS Class locomotives) shunted the remaining Kirtleys to the duplicate list.

No. 17A became the first H&BR locomotive withdrawn, in 1917, being dismantled eventually at Springhead Works, as were 14A, 21A and 31A in 1920. The others lasted until the H&BR merged with the North Eastern Railway, which promptly withdrew all the Kirtley locomotives between 5th June and 27th October 1922. Nos. 22A and 28A were despatched at Springhead, the rest went via Hull Dairycoates Shed to Darlington for scrapping. However Nos. 15A, 23A and 30A were observed passing through Newcastle Central Station in midsummer 1922 on their last journey en route to Percy Main, graveyard of so many tired old engines.

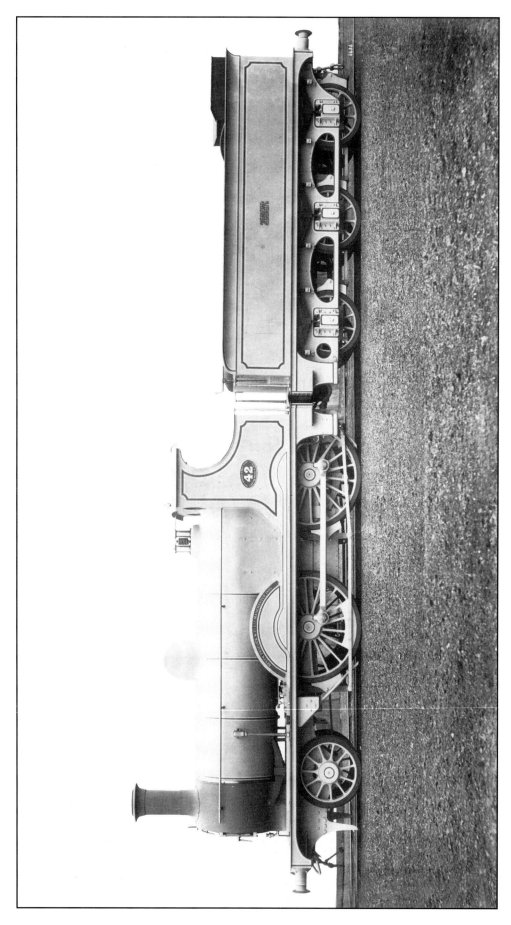

Plate 3 **H&BR Class C 2-4-0 Tender Locomotive, No. 42.** Beyer Peacock works No. 2448. This locomotive was rebuilt with a Stirling pattern 4ft 3in diameter domeless boiler in 1900 and designated class H under the 1908 reclassification scheme.

CLASS C 2-4-0 TENDER LOCOMOTIVES, Nos. 33 – 42

This class of ten neat, typically Victorian locomotives were the only 2-4-0's originated by William Kirtley: all his LC&DR express passenger types being 4-4-0's. Luckily for Kirtley, he didn't have to look far for inspiration, for his predecessor William Martley had left the LC&DR with the most effective express engines south of the Thames in the 1870's: the "Europa" Class of 1873, built specially for working the Government Continental Mail contracts specials. Coincidentally under Kirtley's LC&DR classification, the "Europas" were Class C also.

Basically all Kirtley had to do was update a tried and trusted design - both the "Europas" and H&BR Class C shared the same 7ft 9in + 8ft 3in wheelbase, 17in x 24in cylinders, 140 lb/in² boiler pressure and 4ft 3in diameter boilers. The C Class had leading wheels of 3ft 9in diameter (smaller than the "Europas") and a modern appearance given by mainframes inside, rather than outside the wheels as on the "Europas". The most notable difference was the 6ft driving wheels of the Class C's – 6in smaller than the "Europa" Class. Regarding the late Victoria state of the art locomotive engineering, this made the "Europas" the faster locomotives but could have been worth an extra carriage or two for the H&BR engines.

Other items were common with the Class B: tenders were identical; the Stephenson Link valve gear was fitted with screw reverser (the Class A tanks had a long lever to effect this), and boilers were identical, save for 5in longer barrels on the Class C. (Classes A and B had barrels of similar length; Class A had shorter fireboxes than Classes B and C). An inconsistency in Kirtley's approach to designing the two H&BR tender classes may be noted: the Class B (faced with the heavier work), were handicapped by smaller cylinders and bigger wheels than their Chatham equivalents, but the Class C got considerably smaller wheels than the "Europas". It would seem that Kirtley underestimated the difficulties facing H&BR freight workings, but overestimated them for passenger trains.

As a result, the Class C were able to take a share in working fast goods trains, and photographs exist showing them in service on fish and frozen meat van workings. To balance this the Class B not infrequently hauled heavy passenger trains, excursions, emigrant specials and suchlike.

Like the Class B, the contract with Beyer, Peacock for the ten Class C locomotives was signed on 19th July 1883. Each cost £2,745; all were Westinghouse braked. They were paid for in instalments and none were delivered until some three weeks after the line opened. (Works numbers were 2479-2488).

H&BR passenger workings attracted little attention in the popular railway press, so we have scant information about the workings and performance of the Class C's.

Matthew Stirling stated (in his 1887 lecture), the average weight of H&BR passenger train was 145 tons; expresses averaged 45mph and stopping trains 'ran' at 33mph. The train weights given included around 64³/4 tons for the locomotive and tender, so the following load was about 80¹/4 tons, or 6 carriages. To haul their featherweight loads (a mere third heavier than themselves), the Class C's consumed 932·5 lbs of coal per hour at a firing rate of 57·4 lbs/ft² of grate area, or 23·9 lbs per train mile - somewhat heavy by the standards of 40 years later, but quite reasonable for the 1880's. With coal priced at less than £1 per ton though, one first class passenger literally paid the coal bill.

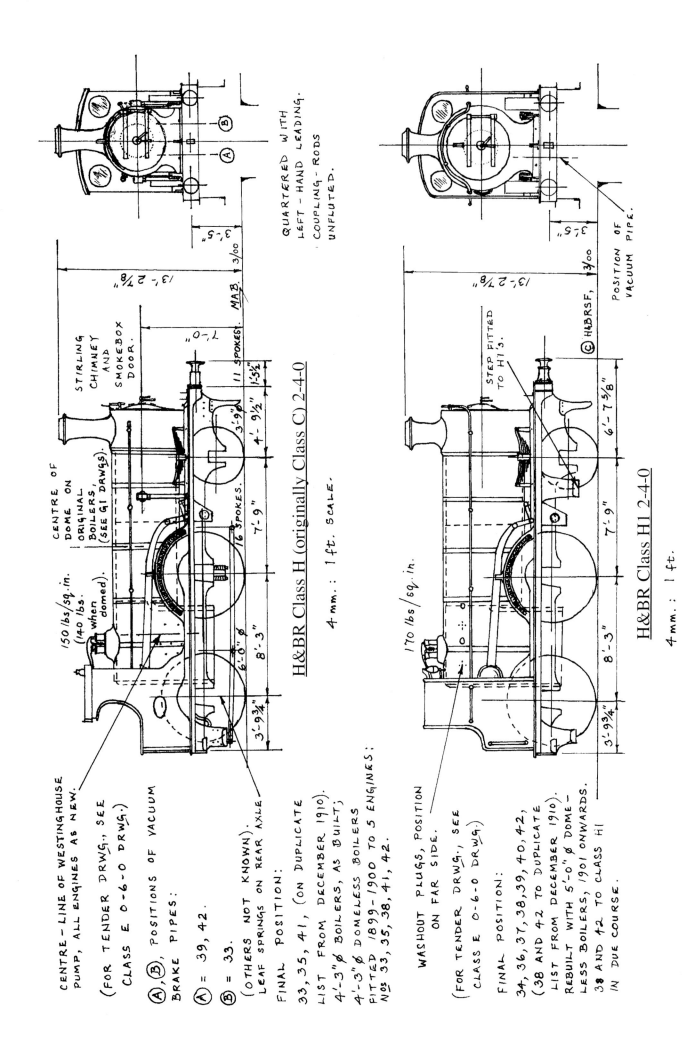

H&BR Class H (originally Class C) 2-4-0

4 mm. : 1 ft. SCALE.

QUARTERED WITH
LEFT-HAND LEADING.
COUPLING-RODS
UNFLUTED.

MAB. 3/00

STIRLING
CHIMNEY
AND
SMOKEBOX
DOOR.

CENTRE OF
DOME ON
ORIGINAL
BOILERS,
(SEE GI DRWGS).

150 lbs/sq.in.
(140 lbs.
when
domed).

CENTRE-LINE OF WESTINGHOUSE
PUMP, ALL ENGINES AS NEW.

(FOR TENDER DRWG., SEE
CLASS E 0-6-0 DRWG.)

Ⓐ, Ⓑ, POSITIONS OF VACUUM
BRAKE PIPES:

Ⓐ = 39, 42.

Ⓑ = 33.

(OTHERS NOT KNOWN).
LEAF SPRINGS ON REAR AXLE

FINAL POSITION:

33, 35, 41, (ON DUPLICATE
LIST FROM DECEMBER 1910).
4'-3"∅ BOILERS, AS BUILT;
4'-3"∅ DOMELESS BOILERS
FITTED 1899-1900 TO 5 ENGINES:
Nᵒˢ 33, 35, 38, 41, 42.

H&BR Class H1 2-4-0

4 mm. : 1 ft.

STEP FITTED
TO H1'S.

POSITION
OF
VACUUM PIPE.

Ⓒ H&BRSF, 3/00

170 lbs/sq.in.

WASHOUT PLUGS, POSITION
ON FAR SIDE.

(FOR TENDER DRWG., SEE
CLASS E 0-6-0 DRWG.)

FINAL POSITION:

34, 36, 37, 38, 39, 40, 42,
(38 AND 42 TO DUPLICATE
LIST FROM DECEMBER 1910).
REBUILT WITH 5'-0"∅ DOME-
LESS BOILERS, 1901 ONWARDS.
38 AND 42 TO CLASS H1
IN DUE COURSE.

Similar modifications were carried out on the Class C's as on the B's; Stirling's reboilering programme taking place from 1899 to 1903. Nos. 33 and 41 (in 1899), 35, 38 and 42 (in 1900), received domeless boilers otherwise similar to the originals but with 150 lb/in² pressure. Kirtley's cabs were retained, but the cylinders were bored out to 17¹/₂in diameter. The other five were rebuilt between 1901 and 1903 with 170 lb domeless boilers with the exceptional diameter of 5 ft 0 in, the largest in Britain at the time. By 1908 the small-boilered locomotives were reclassified as H, those with 5ft diameter boilers becoming Class H1; at some time in the 1900's Nos. 38 and 42 were reboilered to become H1's. The large boilers and new Stirling cabs completely changed the character of the locomotives: from the "mantlepiece ornament" appearance of Class C, the Class H1's acquired a rotund, even distended appearance fully deserving of the nickname 'Jumbos' bestowed on them by their crews.

The Class H and H1 variants took sole charge of the main H&BR Passenger services without distinction between the two: photographs depict both types at the head of various workings on and off the H&BR including the showpiece Sheffield services, complete with new bogie carriages from 1907. They were no strangers to the Peak District, North Wales Coast, Lancashire and the Leeds area on excursions; Class H No. 33A for example regularly worked the Night Mail from 1912 to 1914.

Class H1 No. 34 suffered the H&BR's worst accident. At 7.00pm on 23rd December 1903, a passenger train from Cudworth in bad weather ploughed into the back part of a train at Locomotive Junction, on the outskirts of Hull. A broken coupling resulted in eleven wagons and the brake van being left in No. 34's path, the incompleteness of the coal train being unnoticed by the Junction signalman as it passed him. Only three passengers gave notice of slight injuries, but No. 34's driver was seriously injured. The locomotive suffered extensive superficial damage but was repaired and continued to run until 1922.

1910 saw the introduction of Stirling's five Class J express 4-4-0's, and Nos. 33, 35, 38, 41 and 42 consequently transferred to the duplicate list. In 1917 No. 38A was withdrawn and dismantled at Springhead, the rest soldiered on to he scrapped by the North Eastern. Nos. 40 and 41A were despatched at Springhead before June 1922; between then and October. Nos. 33A-37, 39 and 42A went via Dairycoates to Darlington, although No. 33A at least, ended its life at Percy Main.

Plate 4 **H&BR Brake Third, No. 1.** This was one of only three ordered from Ashburys Railway Carriage & Iron Company. All the Kirtley designed four-wheel passenger carrying stock were built to the same basic body dimensions of 27ft long by 8ft wide carried on a 16ft wheelbase underframe.

THE CARRIAGE STOCK

It was the custom in days of yore for the railway companies to have volumes of drawings referring to their rolling stock. A large company such as the North Eastern had one or maybe two bound volumes dealing with locomotives alone, and another five or six dealt with carriages. Yet more such books dealt with wagons. Initially, the earliest such drawings (or diagrams as they were known 'in the trade'), were crude outlines, without detail. By the 1920's diagrams sported more detail; coupling and connecting rods appeared in line form on locomotive diagrams.

The H&BR were content to use crude, blueprint-type, outline diagrams drawn to a scale of 1/8th inch to 1ft for their locomotives, but generally did much better for their carriage stock. However, whereas order and logic ruled in the locomotive department, the 'systems' used both in carriage numberings and allocation of diagrams exhibited eccentricity to the point of whimsicality. For example by mid 1907 in the carriage stock lists "No. 2" represented variously Brake 3rd of 1885; All 3rd. of 1885; Composite of 1885; Luggage Brake of 1885; Carriage Truck of 1885, Horse Box of 1885 or a Bogie Brake 3rd newly delivered in the February of that year.

Withdrawal and conversion of older stock did go some small way towards eliminating the state of chaos, but not until 1920 did those responsible embark on a complete logical renumbering of all the carriage stock along with the updating, reissuing and renumbering of all the relevant diagrams. In order to try and assist those who may be interested in pursuing further details of H&BR carriage stock, reference has been made only to those diagrams allocated from 1920. To attempt to unravel the conundrum represented by the early H&BR diagram numbers is impossibility, since there is considerable doubt as to whether the H&BR allocated numbers to the carriage and wagon diagrams prior to 1920.

Plate 5 **The carriage shop at the H&BR's Springhead works, c1910.** On the left one of the 1885 Horseboxes is being repaired whilst the overhead crane is engaged in lifting a four-wheel Third on the right. In the background one of the recently built bogie lavatory carriages by Birmingham Railway Carriage & Wagon Co. is being rubbed down.

BRAKE THIRDS, Nos. 1 - 3 (H&BR Diagram 19)

These three vehicles were ordered from Ashburys Railway Carriage & Iron Company of Manchester on 26th February 1885 and were delivered before the end of the year. They were doubtlessly based closely on existing London Chatham & Dover Rly. types by William Kirtley, and can fairly be considered as old-fashioned even by the standards of 1885. After 14 years service, the H&BR board sought tenders for some six-wheeled vehicles, but this move came to nought. Eight more years passed before the Company took delivery of bogie carriages which compared with the best to be found anywhere in the country.

Although the H&BR four-wheelers were somewhat uninspired, they were soundly and solidly built. Details were: Body Length: 27ft, Wheelbase: 16ft, Width: 8ft, length over Headstocks: 26ft 11in. Height inside at centre; 7ft 0in, Doorway heights: 6ft 0in clear. Wooden–segmented wheels of the Mansell type were 3ft 7in diameter. Headstocks; body framing, outside panelling mouldings and doors were of Best Moulmein Teak: solebars of American, Danzig or Stettin Oak. Roofboards were of 7/8in pitch pine, canvas covered and white leaded but finished inside with lincrusta. Buffers were standardised at 5ft 8in centres, 3ft 5in above rail height. Continuous footboards were fitted, plus bottom steps at every door. Pope's Patent Gas lighting was fitted, as were Westinghouse and guard's handbrakes plus Varley's Patent Electrical Communicator, between passengers and guard in case of emergencies. Third Class compartments were 5ft 3in wide, upholstered in rep to 26in above the seats. The guard's compartment was the equivalent of two passenger compartments in size, and contained a ventilated dog box.

Details evident on the photograph are the gas tank pressure gauge on the solebar to the left of the builder's plate, the safety chains fitted to the headstocks in addition to the screw-link coupling; the double lens lamp fitted over the guard's lookout (or ducket in railway parlance), access to the lamp burner being via a small, hinged door inside the guard's compartment. The lettering, of a blocked and shaded Sans-Serif style, remained standard for the remainder of the Company's existence, but the elaborate 'HB&WJR' monogram approximately halfway along the carriage side passed out of use at a comparatively early date.

Brake Third Carriage No. 1 (the subject of the photograph), had a long and active existence. The H&BR, sold it to dealers Edmunds & Radley Ltd. in the Spring of 1919 for £160; they resold it that September to the Neath & Brecon Rly. which put it into service almost immediately with minimal expense. It was eventually withdrawn by the mighty Great Western Railway in October 1925, and sold intact by them. The body was in due course grounded as a shed near Monmouth but was ultimately rescued in 1986 by the Welsh Industrial & Maritime Museum, where it currently awaits restoration.

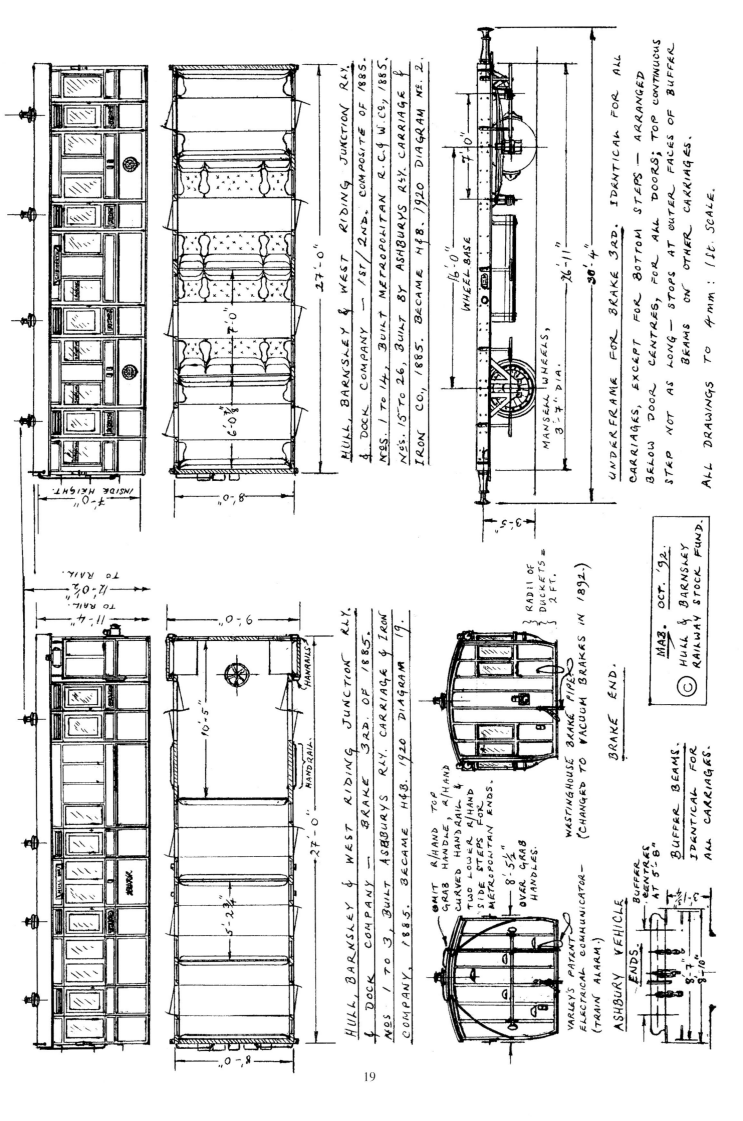

FIRST AND SECOND CLASS COMPOSITES, Nos. 1 - 26 (H&BR Diagram 1)

These twenty-six carriages originated from two sources: the Metropolitan Railway Carriage & Wagon Company produced Nos. 1 to 14 (including No. 11, subject of the photograph), as part of the large contract awarded them in August 1883. The contract for the last twelve went to the Ashburys Railway Carriage & Iron Company in February 1884. The Metropolitan built stock was all delivered by 30th June 1885 whereas the Ashbury vehicles appeared later in the year.

Dimensionally the Composites were similar to the Third Class carriages but with more generously sized compartments, the Seconds being 6ft 0⁷/₈in wide, the Firsts being a spacious 7ft 0in. This meant that four compartments fitted into the standard 27ft body length compared with five in the Thirds, as can be seen by comparing the two photographs.

Not evident of course are the differences in internal finishings and upholstery. The Second Class were upholstered with best woollen rep, the Firsts were resplendent in blue cloth with lace antimacassars: both were lined with sycamore and walnut, the door panels being finished in yellow pine. Floor carpets were patterned with dark borders and the Company's armorial device interwoven - more plush appointments than the lincrusta partition tops and linoleum floors of the Third Class. The insides of the varnished wood doors carried the coach number and compartment class in gold characters, shaded black.

The first big change in the careers of the Composites (discounting the 1891 change from Westinghouse to vacuum brakes), came on 1st January 1892 with the abolition of Second Class travel - the result of the railway system on a national scale having moved towards upgrading Third Class facilities, following the Midland Railway's lead of the 1870's.

The same year saw No. 25 rebuilt as a saloon with a toilet at one end, to 1920 H&BR Diagram No. 3. Another conversion came in 1896 when No. 19 was rebuilt along generally similar lines but its 1920 Diagram No. 5 shows that differences existed mainly in the external doors, varying ones of which were sealed on both sides of each carriage. Following delivery of the new bogie carriages in1910, fourteen Composites were demoted to Thirds during 1912. Those chosen were Nos. 9, 10, 13-18, 20-24 and 26. As each went into Springhead Works for reupholstering, they were converted quite simply; by removing the armrests from the old First Class and altering the lettering designations. The altered vehicles ultimately received Diagram No. 2.

Also following on from approval by the H&BR Board in 1910 was the fitting of steam heating to the remaining composites, As far back as the summer of 1908 the Lancashire & Yorkshire Railway and other companies had voiced objections to including H&BR vehicles in their trains, since they still relied on the old tin canister-type footwarmers.

World War I caused postponement of the H&BR plans to downgrade the Composites, but this process was resumed in 1920 with Nos. 11 and 12 downclassed to Thirds, so that only Nos. 1 to 8 remained as Diagram 1. Most of these vehicles were withdrawn by the North Eastern in 1922, only Nos. 3, 19-22 received NER numbers: 5000 added on to their H&BR numbers. The saloon conversion from No. 19 (renumbered 27 in 1920), became 5001 and survived until 20 December 1930, the others all being condemned on 22 March 1923 after only three months ownership by the London & North Eastern Railway, following the Grouping.

Plate 6 **H&BR 1st/2nd Composite, No. 11.** A total of 26 Composites were ordered; fourteen from Metropolitan Railway Carriage & Wagon Company (Nos. 1-14) whilst the balance of twelve were supplied by Ashburys Railway Carriage & Iron Company.

Plate 7 **H&BR All Third, No. 5.** One of the twenty built by Metropolitan Railway Carriage & Wagon Company. Another 24 were ordered from Ashburys Railway Carriage & Iron Company.

ALL THIRDS, Nos. 1 - 44. (H&BR Diagram 21)

These carriages were tendered for in two lots - by the Metropolitan Railway Carriage & Wagon Company for twenty carriages in August 1883, and a further twenty-four in February 1885 from Ashburys Railway Carriage & Iron Company.

Dimensionally similar to the Brake Thirds and most likely similar to Kirtley's vehicles on the London, Chatham & Dover Rly, the H&BR vehicles improved in one respect at least upon their worst specimens by having full height partitions for seat backs: thereby offering a measure of privacy at the expense of conviviality.

They enjoyed somewhat chequered careers: No. 7 never even entered H&BR service, being sold to their contractors Lucas & Aird, who probably used it for the conveyance of workmen, doubtlessly suffering unduly as a result, a replacement was ordered from Ashburys. Possibly No. 7 was converted into a saloon carriage. As such a vehicle was presented by the contractors to the H&BR and no order for such a vehicle appears in H&BR records, despite the fact that an "Inspecting Carriage" figured in the 1886 Stock List. It has also been noted that Stirling and other Company officers liked the saloon so much that they purloined it for their own use. This could explain lack of a running number for the saloon and its untimely demise being apparently smashed up (presumably accidentally), early in 1895, since it disappeared from the Stock Lists that summer. Inspection carriages tended to pop up in unlikely places in their duties; also by the very nature of the work, numerous minor (but sometimes spectacular), collisions occurred in the confines of locomotive sheds and yards.

1909 saw another saloon, appear, converted from No. 26: a toilet compartment fitted at one end occupied about half the old passenger compartment, the far end doors were retained and longitudinal seats took up both sides, tramcar fashion. This conversion received the 1920 Diagram No. 4.

Mention has already been made of the antiquated nature of the passenger stock, even by 1885 standards. Tentative moves made by the Board in 1899 towards ordering some six-wheeled vehicles proved unproductive, but aspirations of the travelling public rose. In November 1903 (spoilt by corridors, vestibules, electric lights, steam heating, restaurant and sleeping carriages on other companies' trains), one A.K.Dibb, Esq. of Kirk Ella sent an "address" to the H&BR Board, with twenty-two fellow signatories complaining "…as to the inferior and unsafe condition of many of the passenger carriages... The worst are the third class carriages, and there are several of these which we consider absolutely unsafe when passing points or curves". The Board, stung on a sensitive spot, replied tartly that there was, "… no justification…", but public spirited Mr. Dibb, not prepared to let them off the hook too readily, had the last word "We ….wished only to put on record opinion of the bad state of any of your passenger coaches…, we conceived this a duty: we have discharged it, and in doing so we have placed on others a still clearer responsibility". It should be noted that nothing untoward happened as a result of the rough riding Kirtley vehicles, but by 1903 it was no longer usual to find four–wheeled passenger vehicles in express trains.

Mr. Dibb waited three more years for relief in the form of the fine new bogie carriages, which apart from (hopefully), appeasing him had the effect of releasing more four-wheelers from passenger service.

In June 1903 whilst deliberating over the desirability of these new carriages, the Board agreed to convert Nos. 41-44 to Brake Thirds, matching the existing Diagram 19, but without guard's lookouts. Further deliveries of bogie stock in 1909 further affected the Thirds: 7, 22-24 were turned over to various railway works' department usage and a dozen more (25, 27-30, 33-37, 39 and 40), were converted into fruit vans, becoming Diagram 22.

Carriages 21, 31 and 32 were steam-heated but demoted to use by workmen only (as Diagram 21), and No. 8 also saw a change of use being rebuilt into a special saloon (Diagram 20). This for conveying Stirling and several senior staff daily between their workplace at Springhead and Beverley Road Station, Hull, although unless the weather was exceptionally bad Matthew Stirling rode on the locomotive, usually driving it himself. This Saloon also appeared throughout the H&BR system in connection with inspection duties, and when not so engaged was available for hire by outside parties.

So matters remained throughout World War I until early 1919, when the Cardiff Railway bought Nos. 3, 11, 15 and 16 and the Rhymney Railway took Nos. 1, 4 and 19. Probably the Rhymney acted as agents for a South Wales colliery company providing itself with a private train for the workforce: a not uncommon practice before the 1923 Railway Grouping.

The Cardiff Railway converted two carriages into Brake Thirds, one and a half compartments being altered. One was eventually sold to the Bishop's Castle Railway, serving them ten years; at the dismantling of that line its underframe became a rail-carrier whilst the body was sold off as a holiday bungalow on the Cardigan Coast.

Four other Thirds reached South Wales in 1919: rolling stock dealer Edmunds & Radley Ltd bought Nos. 6, 9, 10, 12, and 13 (with Brake Third No. 1 already mentioned), and sold them to the Neath & Brecon Railway on 10 September. Thus it transpired the Great Western Railway acquired substantial numbers of ex-Hull & Barnsley vehicles, condemning the last in November 1930.

Tyneside dealer Watts, Hardy & Co. bought Nos. 2, 5, 14 and 18 in 1919, but they remained in the North East, going to the Harton Coal Company for use on its Marsden, Whitburn & South Shields Railway.

1925 saw the end of nearly all H&BR four-wheeled carriage stock handed over to the London & North Eastern Rly, the last three thirds on the H&BR itself (Nos. 17, 20 and 38), having become workshop vehicles by 1922. Stirling's saloon conversion remained until December 1930, by which time very few four-wheeled carriages survived in regular use on the LNER or anywhere else for that matter.

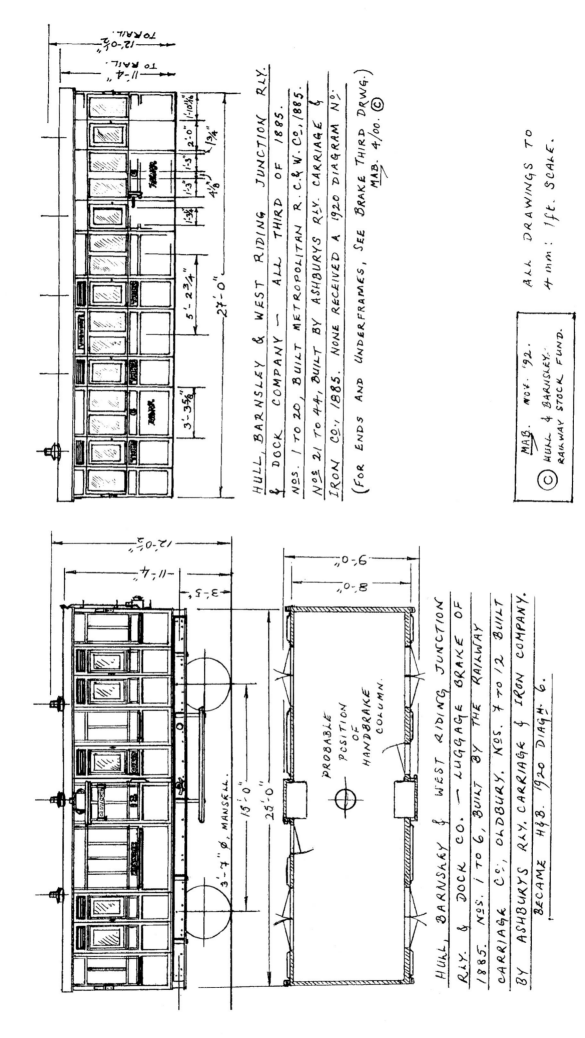

HULL, BARNSLEY & WEST RIDING JUNCTION RLY.
& DOCK COMPANY — ALL THIRD OF 1885.

NOS. 1 TO 20, BUILT METROPOLITAN R. C. & W. Co., 1885.
NOS. 21 TO 44, BUILT BY ASHBURYS RLY. CARRIAGE &
IRON CO., 1885. NONE RECEIVED A 1920 DIAGRAM NO.

(FOR ENDS AND UNDERFRAMES, SEE BRAKE THIRD DRWG.)
MAB. 4/00. ©

HULL, BARNSLEY & WEST RIDING JUNCTION
RLY. & DOCK CO. — LUGGAGE BRAKE OF
1885. NOS. 1 TO 6, BUILT BY THE RAILWAY
CARRIAGE CO., OLDBURY. NOS. 7 TO 12 BUILT
BY ASHBURYS RLY. CARRIAGE & IRON COMPANY.
BECAME H.&.B. 1920 DIAGM. 6.

MAB. NOV. '92.
© HULL & BARNSLEY.
RAILWAY STOCK FUND.

ALL DRAWINGS TO
4mm : 1ft. SCALE.

PROBABLE
POSITION
OF
HANDBRAKE
COLUMN.

PASSENGER LUGGAGE BRAKES, Nos. 1 – 12 (H&BR Diagram 6)

Although it had been recommended to the Board in 1883 that the H&BR would require twenty Passenger Brake Vans, these twelve vehicles sufficed throughout the existence of the Company. Kirtley submitted specifications for these vehicles on 7th December 1883 and early in January 1884 the tender for construction of the first six was awarded to the Ashburys Railway Carriage & Iron Company. The following month saw the Railway Carriage Company (of Oldbury), bid successfully for construction of the final six. The Ashburys vehicles had been completed and delivered to Hull by June 1885, the Oldbury batch appeared by December.

The photograph of No. 12 not only reveals a neat, good looking vehicle, but also that both Oldburys and their photographer had to make the most of a photo opportunity that was rather inopportune. Clearly, at the appointed time No. 12 was not quite finished: items such as axleboxes and springs appear in primer or undercoat, and the Westinghouse brake pipe at the end of the van leans at a drunken angle, having been temporarily loosened and swung over out of the way so that rubbing-down and varnishing can be completed more easily. The bodywork on the side photographed lacks the glossy shine evident on the other carriage photographs, and finally, the lettering is of a style never used on any other H&BR vehicle, being of a Serif type. It would seem therefore that having delivered the earlier vehicles as quickly as possible the Oldbury company had one last chance to get their work's photograph, so No.12 was wheeled out of the paintshop, the lettering possibly temporarily stencilled neatly on one side and having posed for the camera, was then rolled back inside for final attention.

Although generally similar to the carriages, the luggage Brakes were, at 25ft, two feet shorter and had a 15ft wheelbase. They were 8ft wide (9ft over duckets, which were central on each side). The interiors were painted gloss cream, the floors with lead grey.

Apart from the change of continuous brakes in 1891, the vans mostly enjoyed a humdrum existence. In 1905, in connection with the through Hull - Sheffield service, those trains were apparently made up of three of the borrowed Midland Railway Clayton arc-roofed, six-wheelers with an H&BR Van; after the Midland's carriages were returned in April 1906, it is likely that the Luggage Brakes continued in the formations with the H&BR four-wheelers until February 1907 and the delivery of the new bogie carriages.

The Midland Railway hadn't quite finished with the old H&BR vans, however. A surfeit of seasonal bonhomie might explain the early demise of Van No. 3, for (appropriately enough), on Boxing Day 1912 a Midland Railway shunting move at Cudworth was undertaken with more enthusiasm than skill resulting in the unfortunate van being so badly damaged that the H&BR withdrew it in the following year. This was the only occasion, on which an H&BR passenger vehicle was withdrawn due to an accident (except for the probable destruction of the inspection saloon referred to earlier). Nevertheless some of the vans saw considerable use - in October 1910, the Board agreed to steam-heat or through-pipe, four vans "…in regular use with steam-heated vehicles."

1920 saw the luggage Brakes renumbered as 28-38, but upon the 1922 North Eastern merger, further records of the vans disappear. They had either been turned over to departmental use or withdrawn without renumbering by the NER, and thus never appeared in London & North Eastern Railway stock in 1923.

Plate 8 **H&BR Passenger Luggage Brake, No. 12.** This carriage was the last of the batch of six built (Nos. 7–12) by the Railway Carriage Company (of Oldbury). The first batch of six came from Ashburys Railway Carriage & Iron Company. These brake vans were only 25ft long on a wheelbase of 15ft.

Plate 9 **H&BR Horse Box, No. 6.** Built by Metropolitan Railway Carriage & Wagon Company. Though a through pipe was fitted these vehicles were originally un-braked – soon rectified by the fitting of a single-shoe brake and lever.

HORSE BOXES, Nos. 1-10 (H&BR Diagram 15)

It had been decided in April 1883 that the H&BR required thirteen Horse Boxes, like the Luggage Brakes, they were built in two batches by two builders at the same time as the Brakes. This time, the contract for six Horse Boxes went to the Metropolitan Railway Carriage & Wagon Company on 11th January 1884, whilst the final four were ordered from the Railway-Carriage Company of Oldbury at the same time as the last six Luggage Brakes.

The Metropolitan-built Horse Boxes were delivered by 30th June 1885, the four from Oldbury appeared by the end of the year. The vehicles were straight-sided, panelled in tongued and grooved planks and included compartments for the groom, horse and tack; the central compartment was without footboards since horses understandably didn't need them. The groom's compartment was the only one to be given a lamp in the roof: initially most probably of the oil pot variety, since there is no sign of a gas cylinder under the vehicle in the photograph. The slatted panel at the bottom of the groom compartment side was for a ventilated dog-box under the seat.

The Horse Boxes were 19ft in length by 7ft 10in wide; inside height at the centre-line being 7ft 9in, and from floor to under the cantrail, 6ft 9in. The wheelbase was 11ft, and the Mansell wheels (same as the carriages), were 3ft 7in diameter.

A significant omission (as revealed by the works' photograph), was a handbrake, lack of which was soon rectified by Springhead Works, which fitted a single-block Scotch-type brake. This worked on one wheel under the groom compartment, the operating lever pointing to the right and ending under the tack compartment. Some time after 1892 vacuum brakes were fitted, with four blocks arranged to clasp the wheels under the tack compartment, thus giving these vehicles an unusual five-block brake system. Most likely the through Westinghouse pipe was retained, for use on systems using that brake.

During the 1900's the Horse Boxes were rebuilt; the groom and tack compartment doors were replanked vertically, and from 1908 through-piping for steam-heating was fitted following objections from the Lancashire & Yorkshire Railway and other companies, which did not appreciate the antique amenities the H&BR's stock offered. (It should be appreciated that a vehicle without through-piping at the head of a train of steam-heated stock effectively isolated the whole train from the steam provider, ie: the locomotive, thus rendering the train's heating system inoperable).

Renumbering came in 1920, as 64-73, although it is doubtful whether these numbers actually appeared on the vehicles; eighteen months later, the North Eastern added 5000 to the numbers of the H&BR carriage stock. Yet another change of ownership came in 1923 when the London & North Eastern Railway absorbed the North Eastern and renumbered the Horse Boxes into separate lists: Nos. 5065-69 duly became 451-455; 5071-5073 became 457-459. Nos. 5064 and 5070 were condemned without renumbering on 31st March 1924, the others probably didn't last much longer.

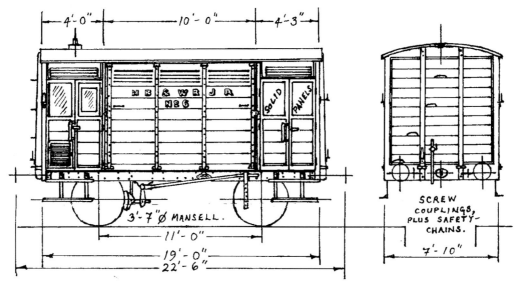

HULL, BARNSLEY & WEST RIDING JUNCTION RLY. & DOCK Cº.
HORSE BOX, OF 1885. Nºs. 1 TO 6 BUILT METROPOLITAN R.C.&W.
Nºs. 7 TO 10 BUILT BY THE RAILWAY CARRIAGE COMPANY. 1920 DIAGRAM Nº· 15.
(SINGLE SCOTCH BRAKE FITTED SOON AFTER DELIVERY. VACUUM CLASP-
    TYPE BRAKES FITTED TO OTHER AXLE, SOON AFTER 1892).   MAB 4/00 ©

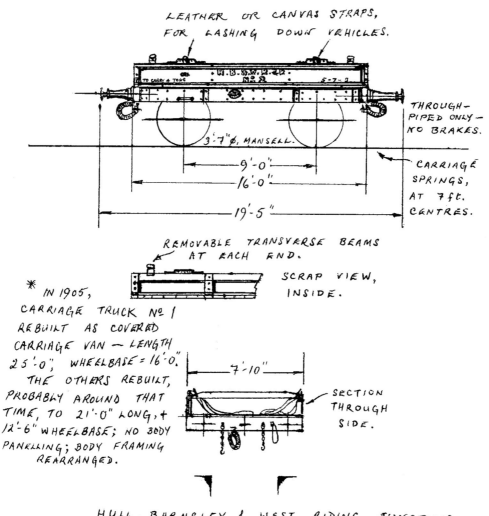

LEATHER OR CANVAS STRAPS,
FOR LASHING DOWN VEHICLES.

THROUGH-
PIPED ONLY -
NO BRAKES.

CARRIAGE
SPRINGS,
AT 7 ft.
CENTRES.

REMOVABLE TRANSVERSE BEAMS
AT EACH END.

SCRAP VIEW,
INSIDE.

* IN 1905,
CARRIAGE TRUCK Nº 1
REBUILT AS COVERED
CARRIAGE VAN — LENGTH
25'-0", WHEELBASE = 16'-0".
THE OTHERS REBUILT,
PROBABLY AROUND THAT
TIME, TO 21'-0" LONG, +
12'-6" WHEELBASE; NO BODY
PANELLING; BODY FRAMING
REARRANGED.

SECTION
THROUGH
SIDE.

HULL, BARNSLEY & WEST RIDING JUNCTION
RLY. & DOCK Cº. — CARRIAGE TRUCK OF 1885.
Nºs. 1 TO 6, BUILT BY CRAVENS BROS., SHEFFIELD.
    BECAME H&B 1920 DIAGᴹ· 16.*

OPEN CARRIAGE TRUCKS, Nos. 1 – 6 (H&BR Diagram 16)

Time was when the landed gentry and other moneyed classes took their own carriages with them on their travels, and in the dawning years of the railway age even travelled in them whilst loaded on carriage trucks. However, improvements in First class standards meant that particular practice died out well before the H&BR opened its platform barriers.

Since that line traversed several estates (notably at Carlton Towers and Hotham, near North Cave), it was obvious that there could be some custom for carriage trucks. Twelve had been recommended, but six only were ordered from Cravens Brothers, Sheffield, on 26th February 1884 and this number was never added to.

They all appeared before the end of the year and were 16ft long, 7ft 10in wide with a 9ft wheelbase. These vehicles had a low, fixed side, 15in high, with shackles at each end for roping down carriages and removable cross-beams at each end to facilitate loading but stiffen up the sides when refitted. Carriage-type Mansell wooden segmental wheels of 3ft 7in diameter were fitted and through-brake pipes allowed the vehicles to run in passenger trains, although the individual Carriage Trucks themselves were unbraked – again a similar omission to the Horse Boxes.

Possibly the transport of motor vehicles and the prospects of petrol leakage plus locomotive sparks providing a mixture which could prove injurious to health, led to Carriage Truck No. 1 being rebuilt as a covered vehicle in 1905. Only some of the ironwork could have been reused, since the rebuilt vehicle was stretched to 25ft in length with an 11ft wheelbase. The others were rebuilt as opens, but to a length of 21ft on a 12ft 6in wheelbase, probably around the same time.

1908 saw all six trucks through-piped for steam-heat as a result of the objections of the L&YR and others to the H&BR's vehicles (as outlined in the Horse Box section).

The last few years of the existence of the Carriage Trucks saw them renumbered in 1920: Nos. 2-6 became 74-78, No. 1 became 79. The North Eastern added 5000 to those numbers in 1922, but the year after saw the LNER renumber the Carriage Trucks in separate lists (as with the Horse Boxes). This meant that No. 5076 became 250, and 5078 became 252. The odd one out, the Covered Carriage Truck rebuild of 1905, received the number 253. Nos. 5074, 5075 and 5077 never received their allocated LNER numbers being condemned on 31st March 1924, and it is unlikely that the others long outlived them.

Plate 10 **H&BR Open Carriage Truck, No. 2.** A batch of six were built by Cravens Brothers. This design was un-braked like the horseboxes and only had a through pipe.

BREAKDOWN TRAIN RIDING VAN, No. 1

The next three vehicles could be considered as a set, for together with a 10 ton hand-powered crane they comprised the H&BR's breakdown train. However, since they are pictured individually and at some time between the 1930's and 1950's they were split up and went their own ways, it is more convenient to deal with the history of each vehicle as an individual unit.

One thing which Kirtley knew plenty about was the deployment of a breakdown train; the London, Chatham & Dover Railway was renowned for its lamentable record regarding accidents. It staged so many minor (but occasionally quite nasty), mishaps that in Cockney circles at least it was awarded the appellation 'London, Smash'em and Turnover.' Thankfully this was one aspect in which the H&BR most definitely did not follow the LC&DR.

Still, the H&BR board prepared for untoward happenings by authorising Kirtley to prepare specifications for a breakdown train on 26th February 1885, and in due course, on 24th April the tender of the Metropolitan Railway Carriage & Wagon Company was accepted to produce one Riding Van, a Tool Van and Guard Truck at a total cost of £498 15s 0d. Each van was 25ft long with a 15ft wheelbase, and as can be seen were straight sided, vertically planked. Half of Van No. 1 (the Riding Van), had seats, tables and a brake column, the other half comprised a compartment for the shedmaster (in charge of the crew when on duty), a food store and cast iron cooking stove.

The train duly made its appearance at the various mishaps on the line - notably at the 1903 Locomotive Junction collision, when the unfortunate locomotive No. 34 had to be dragged back to the rails from its resting place at the foot of the embankment. Locomotive Junction kept the breakdown gang busy, since any locomotive which ran away westwards from the sheds or works inevitably crashed through the stops at the end of the headshunt and dived off the embankment, ending up in the lane near the Corporation's Pumping Station. This happened in December 1906 when a driver over-ran signals; the engine ended up on its side in the lane but the crew, abandoning their charge in its flight, landed safely but messily in the settling pond for the shed water-softening plant. Both driver and fireman emerged completely plastered with white sludge. Once again, early in 1909 Stirling tank engine No. 68 trundled away unattended from Springhead Shed and landed in the customary place. Another call-out took the train down the Denaby Branch south of Wrangbrook Junction, when Stirling 0-6-0 goods engine No. 96 ran into a landslide.

Eventually Van No. 1 became North Eastern Rly. No. HB5007 and finally LNER No. 902621. Although the crane and guard truck seem to have parted company with the rest of the train at an earlier date, both Vans 1 and 2 remained as a pair until the mid-1950's at least. By 1969 No. 1 had become isolated near the lockpit at King George V Dock, in Hull. At this point the Hull & Barnsley Railway Stock Fund (which had already purchased a 1910 bogie carriage) made enquiries about purchasing Van 1, since the site it occupied was be cleared pending construction of Queen Elizabeth II Dock. Upon being approached, BR denied all knowledge of the van's ownership, referring the Stock fund to the Docks Board. It became evident that negotiations were taking a turn for the worst when the Docks Board also denied ownership, suggesting that BR be contacted. The contractors for the new dock were not so concerned about the niceties of ownership however, and in their eagerness to clear the site set the unfortunate vehicle ablaze. The Stock Fund were at least able to save the brake column from the ashes and resurrect it, phoenix-like, in their bogie carriage; the contractors,' "Sorry about that," and the eventual opening of Queen Elizabeth Dock came as rather poor recompense.

Plate 11 **H&BR Breakdown Train Riding Van No. 1.** All three breakdown train vehicles were built by Metropolitan Railway Carriage & Wagon Company. The left hand end of this vehicle had seats, tables and a brake column whilst the right hand half was fitted out with a cooking stove and food store.

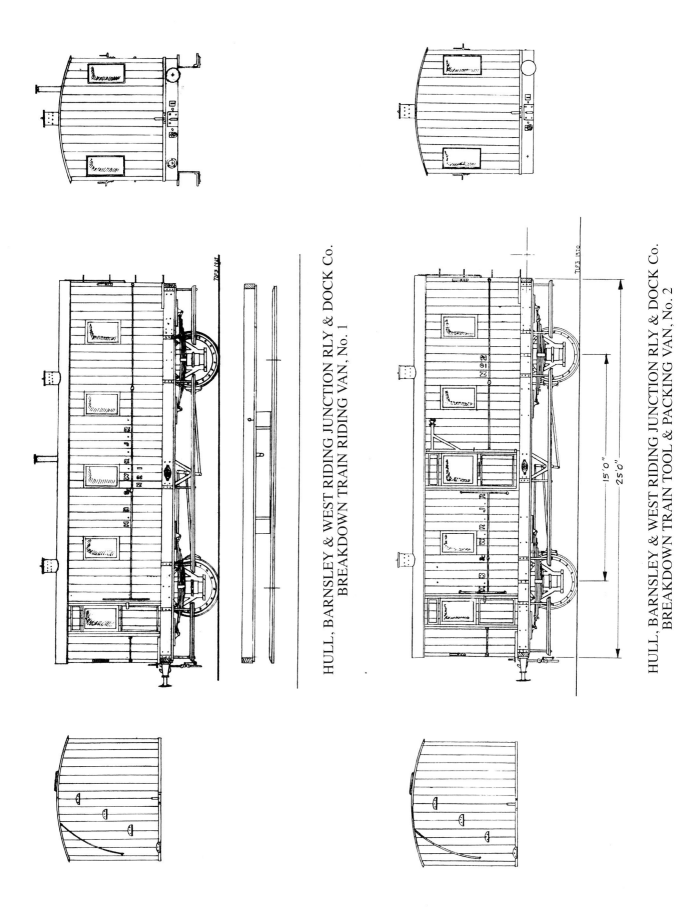

HULL, BARNSLEY & WEST RIDING JUNCTION RLY & DOCK Co.
BREAKDOWN TRAIN RIDING VAN, No. 1

HULL, BARNSLEY & WEST RIDING JUNCTION RLY & DOCK Co.
BREAKDOWN TRAIN TOOL & PACKING VAN, No. 2

Plate 12 **H&BR Breakdown Train Tool and Packing Van No. 2.** The gibbet like arrangement by the door was fitted for unloading jacks, baulks and other heavy re-railing equipment – this device was fitted to both on both sides of the van.

BREAKDOWN TRAIN TOOL AND PACKING VAN, No. 2

Van No. 2 was an important part of the H&BR's breakdown train, being designed to store and transport heavy items such as jacks, hardwood baulks, sheets of old boilerplate, ropes, slings, chains, pulley blocks and so on. Heavy jacks in the 1880's were hand worked, needing at least three men to lug the things around let alone operate them, but did not have the tendency to leak 'off' as modern hydraulic equipment is apt to do unless properly serviced. Hardwood blocks and sleepers would be used to build supports during a lift on soft or uneven ground; old, thick plates with a good coating of grease were put under derailed wheels to 'skid' them across to more convenient positions for rerailing. Plates were also useful to help build ramps up which vehicles could be dragged hack on the rails. To help unload and reload all this gear, the gibbet-like arrangements beside the doors would doubtless prove very useful, and it was this unusual feature which helped to ensure Van 2's survival.

It's career until the 1950's or early '60's paralleled that of Van No. 1, save that it received the NER No. HB5008 and eventually LNER. No. 901622. From then on however, Van 2, eschewing the sedentary habits assumed by its companion No.1, continued a nomadic existence into the 1970's as the Hull Area gasfitters' mobile workshop. As such, it was 'spotted' at Goole by eagle-eyed Hull & Barnsley Railway Stock Fund members early in 1969, the 'gibbets' beside the doors providing initial identification. From then on over the next few months Stock Fund members kept an eye on it, and understandably in view of Van 1's untimely departure from this world in a blaze of glory were dismayed when it suddenly left Goole and effectively vanished for nearly a year. When found it had literally been under their noses all along, having been shunted into Hull Paragon Engineers' Yard virtually underneath Park Street Bridge. Van 2 remained there until early 1973 but its next move was its last under BR ownership, being only three or four miles from Paragon to Priory Yard - with other vehicles waiting to be condemned. Immediate enquiries of the local BR carriage & Wagon Repair Department at Dairycoates revealed that Van 2 was for disposal and in due course the Stock Fund became its fifth owners, for £180.

It was initially planned to move Van 2 to the Humberside Locomotive Preservation Group's siding at Dairycoates for restoration, but since it came with a 'One Journey Only' ticket it was decided to take full advantage of that to move it straight away, to its intended home on the North Yorkshire Moors Railway, with the other Stock Fund vehicles. It was also felt that once off BR's lines they may have been most unwilling to move it again: it should perhaps be pointed out here that at the time of purchase Van 2 was the oldest vehicle on BR and was largely unchanged from its original condition. Replacement doors in an architectural style best described as Victorian Cottage Privy were the main alteration in appearance, and an odd buffer housing bore mute witness to the effects of a long - forgotten rough shunt. Van 2 was also still on its original Mansell wooden wheels, to the astonishment of the BR Wagon Inspector who came to pass it fit to travel to the North Yorkshire Moors Rly. (his blessing was duly received - with the proviso that it did not go 'over the Hump' at Thornaby Marshalling Yard; the effects of the retarder gear getting a grip on 87-year old wooden wheels may be left to the imagination.....). Ultimately the old van left Hull on the overnight freight to Tees Yard, Thornaby, thence on the still extant weekly pickup freight to Whitby and a new life in North Yorkshire.

Initially the van travelled down the Moors line to Pickering, for use by the Late Ted Smith and his assistants as a store van during the restoration of his locomotive "Meteor". With "Meteor's" return to steam Van 2 joined the other Stock Fund vehicles at Goathland, undergoing some restoration work and being put to use as the NYMR's Carriage Department Electrical Stores, a role it fulfils to this day.

BREAKDOWN TRAIN CRANE RUNNER WAGON, No. 3

This particular vehicle was ordered simultaneously with Vans 1 and 2 from the Metropolitan Railway Carriage & Wagon Company. Like the two vans it was one of a pair but in this case its 'twin' was a ten tons capacity, hand powered crane which arrived later from Cowans, Sheldon & Company, at a cost of £430.

Crane Runner Wagon No. 3 had some unusual features which distinguished it from contemporary wagons: the screw couplings and safety chains at each end, long van-type springs and Mansell wheels should he noted. The wagon's sides dropped down over their full length to make it easier for the breakdown crew to unload the impedimenta such as slings, strops, chains, hooks, packing and rail clamps associated with the crane. A feature missing from Wagon No. 3 and usually found on such vehicles was a trestle like cradle for the crane jib to rest upon when travelling, although such a feature was later fitted by the H&BR.

The crane itself ran on six-spoked wheels and had a stoutly made wooden jib, hexagon in cross section and tapering towards the ends. Loads were counterbalanced by an iron box full of weights, which could be run outwards to the rear of the crane on four small, flanged wheels bearing upon the rearward extended bed of the crane, as if on rails. No shelter for the operators was fitted, and adjustment of the angle of the jib must have been a laborious occupation due to the primitive nature of the mechanism provided.

Despite attendance at the occasional mishaps No. 3 and the crane saw most usage in far less spectacular service. The H&BR's station yards were not provided with cranes, although the goods sheds had hoists built into them. Consequently any heavy lifts involved the stationmaster concerned telegraphing Springhead to request the use of the crane.

At the time of the amalgamation with the North Eastern in 1922 we find that although the vans and runner wagon retained their original numbers, the Crane became No. 7. (The missing numbers 4, 5 and 6 were occupied by an open packing wagon built by the H&BR at Cudworth in 1907, a tool van converted from an 1885 covered van No. 474, and a tool van built in 1910 by the H&BR and kept at Alexandra Dock). No. 3 became HB5009 under the LNER, the Crane being renumbered as C.M.E. 21 HB.

By the time of withdrawal in the 1950's, the crane carried the number 901549; no number was evident on the runner wagon, so presumably it was regarded simply as an appendage of the Crane.

Plate 13 **H&BR Breakdown Train Crane Runner Wagon No. 3.** It is painted in the same style as the breakdown train vans in brown. A cradle for the jib of the 10 Ton crane supplied by Cowans Sheldon was fitted later.

Plate 14 **H&BR Five Plank Open Wagon, No. 107.** 225 such wagons were built by Lancaster Wagon Co. Grease axleboxes and two shoe brakes fitted to one side of the wagon were common to railways at this period. Note the carrying capacity and tare painted in italic script and the ironwork picked out in black (the latter is probably only for photographic purposes).

THE GOODS VEHICLES

The traditional British railway goods wagon had a long - too long a career, appearing on the Liverpool & Manchester Railway in the 1830s as the result of bitter experience. The old high-sided, unsprung 2 tons capacity coal wagon as used on the early horse wagonways proved almost useless as a general cargo carrier, and as a result of increasing claims for damaged goods and heavier bills for wagon repairs the Liverpool & Manchester gradually evolved a platform some 12ft long and 7ft wide, on four sprung wheels with drawgear and buffers likewise sprung, plus a simple one-side lever arrangement applying a 'parking' brake. By the 1850's wheelbases had increased from a third of the wagon's length to around 9ft, giving steadier riding, and vehicles had become more specialised: covered vans, low-sided, high-sided and bolster wagons had appeared. There matters rested until the 1900's, save for the introduction of iron then steel underframes instead of wood by the more go-ahead companies, and standardisation of construction methods laid down by the Railway Clearing House in 1887.

By the turn of the century it was obvious to any railway engineer that the increasingly stronger rails laid by then were only taken full advantage of by the locomotives. The heaviest were exerting some ten tons weight per wheel whereas the dear old British wagon even fully laden scarcely approached half that amount, the heaviest bogie carriages coming around halfway between the two. The North Eastern Railway produced a fleet of splendid 40-ton capacity steel hopper bogie coal wagons in 1902 only because the Ashington Coal Company co-operated in modernising its own facilities. At a slightly earlier date, the H&BR struck its own modest blow in the struggle for cost-effective goods stock by introducing longer open wagons. These were unusual in being some 18ft 6in long with a wheelbase of 13ft 6in. It had been found that a wheelbase of 14ft was too long for weighbridges, wagon turntables and the like. This thus demonstrating the main reason for the survival of the British goods wagon: the infrastructure of factories, yards, workshops, collieries, etc., had developed piecemeal from early Victorian times and now constrained the further growth of the wagon. The fact that many non-railway companies maintained their own private wagon fleets hampered the fitting of continuous brakes (many wagons would have to be fitted with a dual/air vacuum brake system anyway), so unfitted goods train speeds remained very low. The length and weight of such trains became limited to what a locomotive could stop, rather than what it could pull. It should consequently come as no surprise to find that the eight-coupled freight engine appeared as late as the 1890's in Britain or that another fifty years were to pass before ten-coupled freight engines appeared in force. Meanwhile a faintly ludicrous and uniquely British situation arose; in which Britain's best express engines were considerably bigger and heavier than main line freight locomotives. In continental Europe both types were about equal in size, weight and power, whereas in the USA the situation was the exact opposite of that in Britain.

Oddly enough, the H&BR followed the American trend. Its biggest locomotive type was the eight-coupled Class A Stirling mineral engine of 1907; at 101 tons, a handsome heavyweight some 46 tons more than Stirling's Class J express passenger engines.

The advent of diesels on the H&BR section remaining in Hull in 1967 showed that old lessons needed relearning, for it was found that the six-wheeled Class 95xx Paxman diesel-hydraulics, transferred from Cardiff had, like the Glaswegian police, to go round in pairs to ward off trouble and guarantee a halt smoothly at, rather than a rough one in, Alexandra Dock.

FIVE PLANK OPEN WAGON, Nos. 1 – 225 (H&BR Wagon Diagram 2)

In view of circumstances outlined in the previous section, Kirtley had neither incentive nor reason to depart from the established norm, so much so that like the passenger stock his goods vehicles seemed to be twenty years behind the times both in size and appearance.

The 1883 Rolling Stock Committee recommended a total of 1,300 wagons the first orders were for 530 vehicles to be delivered in 1885 and tenders would have been invited early in 1884 along with those for the passenger stock. The figure of 1,300 vehicles was reached in the mid-1890's, but by the time of the merger with the North Eastern in 1922 the H&BR contributed 4,535 wagons.

No. 107 was a five-plank open wagon of ten tons capacity, one of 225 built by the Lancaster Wagon Company. Its measurements were 15ft 6in by 7ft 6in on a 9ft wheelbase. The underframes of oak consisted of headstocks 13¹/₂in x 4·4in and solebars 11in x 4¹/₂in faced with steel plates 5/16ins thick. This made a neat job of the external faces of the solebars: since the underframes were largely held together with threaded tie-rods, it saved the necessity of providing each and every rod-end nut with individual plates or washers, although recourse to that method was undertaken in both World Wars in order to save steel and to some extent, labour. Dimensions of the underframes were common to nearly all the wagon stock, and they conformed generally to the Railway Clearing House specifications mandatory from 1887.

All the open wagon bodies had sides of 2¹/₂in thick deal, 2ft 11in high. Items of ironwork visible in the photograph include side hooks and end cleats for roping down wagon sheets, label racks, and handles for use in capstan or horse shunting. Other noteworthy items are the grease-type axleboxes and the single-side, two-block type brake. Both reveal the primeval nature of the British goods wagon.

The grease axlebox consisted of two chambers, divided horizontally by the axle bearing - brass itself. The lower of the two chambers was occupied by the axle end-journal, the upper formed a hollow box with a hinged lid, creating a reservoir which was stuffed with grease. This was usually some vile concoction of tallow, palm oil, water and washing soda, simmered on a moderate heat for several hours and served cool. The stuff melted when warm, a situation occurring in axleboxes as bearings heated up after travelling some miles. The grease gradually trickled down through holes and channels in the bearing brass to lubricate the journal: a crude but effective system. The rolling resistance must have been high and the practice of reducing the surface area of a bearing by having it resemble a slice of Jarlsberg cheese is now unacceptable.

The single-side brake was an abomination and must nave been cursed roundly by generations of wagon shunters, yet only in 1911 did the Board of Trade require the fitting of either-side brakes. These were to be phased in over 15 years in the case of the owners of the largest wagon fleets, ten years in the case of the H&BR. However, due to the activities of one Kaiser Wilhelm II, single-side brakes were still occasionally fitted. In 1918 and could he observed on the main lines into the 1930's.

The early H&BR wagons such as No. 107 were rebuilt from 1902, most being largely unaltered but some emerging rebuilt to a length of 18ft 6in. Rebuilding would have given them a new lease of life for 20 to 30 more years, before scrapping or sale for private use on the internal railway systems of dockyards, collieries, etc. One such was No. 85, which survived at Foster Mills in Norwich until the early 1970's before being presented to the Quainton Railway Society. Due to work of a higher priority No. 85 received little attention other than from the weather, although it is hoped to restore its remains for eventual display: a worthwhile aim, since wagons of that era are extremely rare.

Plate 15 **H&BR Three Plank Dropside Wagon, No. 229.** One of 75 such vehicles built by Brown, Marshall & Co.

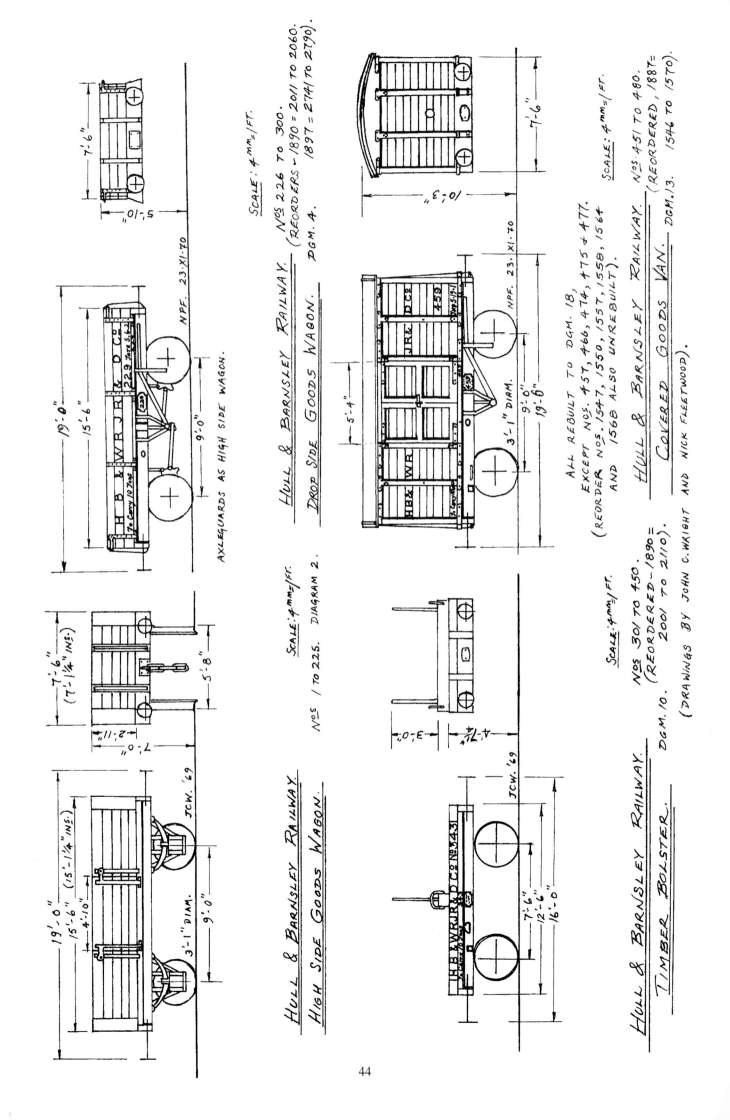

NPF. 23·XI·70

7'-6"

5'-10"

SCALE: 4 mm = / FT.

HULL & BARNSLEY RAILWAY. N⁰S 226 TO 300.
(REORDERS ~1890 = 2011 TO 300.
1897 = 2741 TO 2790).
DGM. A.

DROP SIDE GOODS WAGON.

H B & W R J R & D C⁰

19'-0"
15'-6"
9'-0"

22 9 Tare 5·6·2
7× Carry 10·7ᴺ⁰ˢ
220

AXLEGUARDS AS HIGH SIDE WAGON.

7'-6"
(7'-1¼" INS.)
5'-8"

2'-11"
7'-0"

19'-0"
15'-6" (15'-1¼" INS.)
4'-10"
9'-0"
3'-1" DIAM.

JCW. '69

HULL & BARNSLEY RAILWAY.
HIGH SIDE GOODS WAGON.

SCALE: 4 mm = / FT.
N⁰S. 1 TO 225. DIAGRAM 2.

10'-3"

7'-6"

SCALE: 4 mm = / FT.

5'-4"

NPF. 23. XI·70

3'-1" DIAM.
9'-0"
19'-6"

J R & D C⁰
459
H B & W R
5× Carry 10·7ᴺ⁰ˢ

ALL REBUILT TO DGM. 18,
EXCEPT N⁰S. 457, 466, 474, 475 & 477.
(REORDER N⁰S. 1547, 1550, 1557, 1558, 1564
AND 1568 ALSO UNREBUILT).

HULL & BARNSLEY RAILWAY. N⁰S. 451 TO 480.
(REORDERED, 1887 =
1546 TO 1570).
COVERED GOODS VAN.   DGM. 13.

3'-0"
4'-7¼"

JCW. '69

SCALE: 4 mm = / FT.
N⁰S 301 TO 450.
(REORDERED ~1890 =
2001 TO 2110).

7'-6"
12'-6"
16'-0"

J. H. B. & W R J R & D C⁰ N⁰ 343

JCW. '69

HULL & BARNSLEY RAILWAY.
TIMBER BOLSTER.   DGM. 10.

(DRAWINGS BY JOHN C. WRIGHT AND NICK FLEETWOOD).

44

THREE PLANK DROPSIDE WAGON, Nos.226 – 300 (H&BR Wagon Dia. 4)

No. 229 was one of 75 low-sided wagons built by Brown, Marshall & Co, Ltd., of Birmingham. Basically similar to the five-plank high-sided wagons, they differed only inasmuch as the sides were 1ft 9in deep; instead of a central drop-door, the entire wagon side could be lowered.

The low-sided wagon was probably the closest to the original Liverpool & Manchester type. On that railway almost everything was carried by such wagons, including livestock - see later. However, experience taught the railways that low-sided wagons were mainly useful for carrying bulky items such as cotton or woollen bales, or heavy items like machinery or scrap iron. Bales and machinery would naturally be sheeted down under a tarpaulin, but obviously such precautions were unnecessary for scrap.

Doubtless these 75 wagons had a similar existence to the high-sided wagons but far fewer (if any), would have passed into private ownership upon withdrawal. The H&BR added to a few of the Kirtley wagon types as well as introducing new designs. The 75 dropside wagons were augmented in 1890 by a virtually identical batch from the Metropolitian Railway Carriage & Wagon Co., (Nos. 2011-2060). These were followed up seven years later with another order (Nos. 2741-2790), this time from Hurst Nelson & Co., of Motherwell.

SINGLE BOLSTER WAGONS, Nos. 301 - 450 (H&BR Wagon Dia. 10)

The single bolster wagon was one of the most useful specialist railway goods vehicles. They could be used in pairs, threes or even fours to transport long items such as rails, girders, pipes, masts, etc. The bolster itself could be removed and the wagon used as a spacing vehicle to clear an overhanging load, or between others to provide flexibility at the centre. In the latter case the vertical pins were removed but the bolster itself was sometimes in place to provide support.

These 150 wagons built by the Lancaster Wagon Company, were shorter by three feet than the open wagons and two inches wider, with a wheelbase of 7ft 6in. The bolster measured 9in x 11in, and as can be seen the brake lever applied two blocks, although No.143 was rebuilt in 1914 with four brake blocks and levers on both sides.

Not surprisingly with the large amount of timber traffic from Scandinavia and Russia likely to come through the H&BR's Alexandra Dock, 150 single-bolster wagons would hardly prove adequate and one of Matthew Stirling's first tasks on assuming control in May 1885 was to augment the wagon fleet. This task kept him occupied into 1887, and not surprisingly he drew heavily on his Great Northern Railway training. Fifty double-bolster wagons with a 12ft wheelbase and of largely Great Northern Inspiration appeared by 1887, plus 100 flat wagons for the carriage of squared or sawn timber. (Other early additions to the H&BR's wagon fleet were 40 open fish trucks, 25 meat vans, 150 single-plank flat wagons and 350 9ft 6in high-sided, four-plank open wagons of which one, No. 577 of 1886, has been preserved by the Hull & Barnsley Railway Stock Fund).

Further additions to the wagon stock were largely to the same designs or adaptations of them: very few new designs followed. An indication of the importance of timber traffic to the H&BR is that from Kirtley's initial modest order for 150 single-bolsters, the total passed on to the NER in 1922 came to 440 timber wagons of all types.

Plate 16   **H&BR Single Bolster Wagon, No. 343.** Only 150 single bolsters were ordered from Lancaster Wagon Co. – considering the timber traffic which was imported through the docks at Hull it is not surprising that Matthew Stirling soon added fifty Double Bolster Wagons.

COVERED GOODS VANS, Nos. 451 - 480 (H&BR Wagon Diagram 13)

The covered van appeared in the late 1840's and although offering the immediate advantages of freedom from weather damage, savings on the cost of tarpaulins and greater security from pilfering since they were readily lockable, far too many loads deserving of protection were still carried in open or on flat wagons, even into the 1960's.

Kirtley ordered a mere thirty of these vans from Brown, Marshall & Co. Ltd., of Birmingham, and as can be seen they were limited in size and capacity. The heavy outside body-framing gave them an ancient aspect, added to by the single-side brake, which left the underfloor area looking distinctly 'spindly' by modern standards.

Stirling's designs for additional vans were initially little more modern or substantial in appearance and of similar capacity to earlier vehicles, although by 1922 the H&BR had increased its van fleet to 406 of all types, including insulated, refrigerated meat and fish vans; these later vehicles were considerably larger. Meanwhile, Stirling re-ordered twenty-five vans to Kirtley's design in 1888 from Stableford & Co., (Nos. 1546-1570). These differed from the originals in having a single-side, single-block Scotch-type brake, economy being uppermost in the minds of the H&BR Board at that time, their Company being in receivership. These, and the earlier Kirtley vans had 3ft 1in spoked wheels, springs 3ft 6in long and three-link couplings. The next orders of vans retained the same dimensions as their predecessors, but had louvred ventilators in their upper sides and ends, plus torpedo type roof ventilators, which mark them out as Stirling vehicles.

From 1902, the H&BR's Wagon Shops at Springhead began a rebuilding programme of the early vans, although it was 1910 before the Kirtley originals took their turn. One was rebuilt as original, whereas twenty-five were rebuilt completely, to a new larger type with vertical, flush-planked sides. Four were never rebuilt at all. The Stirling re-order vans were similarly dealt with: eighteen to Springhead's new design, three as original and four remaining unrebuilt. The new type was referred to as Diagram 18 under Springhead's 1920 scheme.

By the 1930's the early Kirtley vans were coming to the end of their lives, although World War II brought difficulties of replacement and caused a postponement of further withdrawals of older vans. Under BR, remaining H&BR vans were cleared off the system in the 1950's, but one Diagram 18 van actually lasted into the 1980's on the military railway which served the gun range at Shoeburyness, near Tilbury. It had been sold off by the LNER in the 1930's, but failed to survive the closure of the gun range railway system.

Plate 17 **H&BR Covered Goods Van, No. 459.** Built by Brown, Marshall & Co. Comparison to LC&DR designs reveals that Kirtley reused an existing design built for the LC&DR (with changes to the brakegear). Many examples were rebuilt in the period after 1910.

CATTLE VANS, Nos. 481 – 500 (H&BR Wagon Diagram 19)

Inspection of old prints of Liverpool & Manchester Railway trains in the mid-1830's show the first departures from the four-wheeled flat wagon for the carriage of livestock. Initially, removable side extensions were fitted to the flat wagons to enable animals to be carried, the unfortunate beasts being accompanied by herders or drovers who needless to say, were not always successful in lashing their hapless charges into submission. The more spirited kine or swine (doubtless encouraged by the odd red-hot cinder ejected from the locomotive chimney) would frequently leap off and display a clean pair of hooves (or trotters), as they headed off into the wide blue yonder and the promise of freedom. Sometimes they came to a sad and gory end under the wheels, such self-sacrifice causing derailments and the wholesale escape of their fellows.

Double-deck cages for sheep soon appeared, but it was some years before covered cattle vans were built, obviating the need for drovers to travel. Thus evolved a vehicle, which has now disappeared from the metals of Britain's railways, its function being taken over completely by road transport offering true door-to-door service. The railway cattle van was used on an individual basis for single loads of a few beasts, or in block trains. In this context, the writer recalls the miles of sidings, platforms and cattle vans near Miles Platting, Manchester, in connection with the Irish cattle trade.

Kirtley provided the H&BR with twenty cattle vans built by Brown, Marshall & Co. Ltd. They were, with a 10ft wheelbase and body 18ft x 8ft, considerably larger than the covered vans although still with only a single brake lever. Another ten cattle vans (Nos. 1571-1580) had entered service in 1888 and a final ten (Nos. 4101-4110) were built by R.Y. Pickering & Co. of Wishaw in 1907. Comparison of photographs reveal that in this instance, Stirling was quite content to reuse Kirtley's design on both occasions, but the last batch were through piped for vacuum brake and steam heating, allowing their use with passenger stock if required. The axle boxes were also modified, being exchanged for more modern oil-lubricated type; thus it would be entirely appropriate to say they were 'beefed-up' – this last delivery of cattle vans were accordingly given diagram 20. Through-piping may well have been applied retrospectively to the earlier batches. Van No. 474 was probably not so equipped since it underwent conversion by the H&BR to a tool van and was re-numbered 5, after the Breakdown Train vehicles and an open packing wagon built at Cudworth in 1907.

It may be worth pointing out that a Cattle van would not have remained in the pristine condition depicted in Brown, Marshall's official photograph, since its passengers were not renowned for their sanitary habits. At the end of each period of occupancy the vans were swilled out and as a further precaution against the spread of infection, it was the custom to paint the two or three planks inside with a wash of quicklime. Liberal applications of the stuff ran out between the planks and on to the running gear below, giving the vehicles a distinctly piebald appearance.

8-Ton GOODS BRAKE VANS, Nos. 1 - 30 (H&BR Wagon Diagram 22)

Appropriately enough, we end our review of the H&BR's earlier stock with the vehicle once found inevitably at the end of every goods train: the humble brake van. These were another uniquely British railway feature, for continental Europe favoured small cabins precariously perched high up on the ends of wagons, and the North American equivalent, the caboose, provided living accommodation as well as brake power, journeys there were measured in thousands of miles.

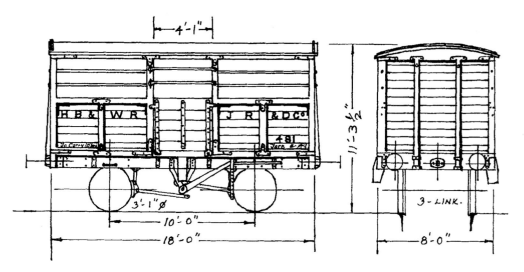

HULL & BARNSLEY RAILWAY.   Nº S. 481 TO 500.
                                (REORDERS - 1888 = 1571 TO 1580)
CATTLE VAN.   DGM. 19.   MAB. 4/00. ©

DRAWINGS TO 4mm: 1ft SCALE.

Nº S. 3 TO 30 UPRATED TO 10 TONS, 1886.   Nº S. 6 TO 30 BUILT
                                            WITHOUT STOVES.

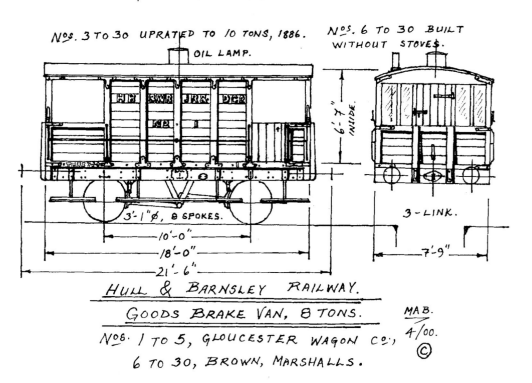

HULL & BARNSLEY RAILWAY.
GOODS BRAKE VAN, 8 TONS.   MAB.
                                        4/00.
Nº S. 1 TO 5, GLOUCESTER WAGON Cº;
6 TO 30, BROWN, MARSHALLS.   ©

Mr. Kirtley presented drawings and specifications to the H&BR Directors on 7th December 1881, and the first order was placed in January 1884. The first six were built by the Gloucester Carriage & Wagon Co. One of these six was sold on to Lucas & Aird, the H&BR contractors, so an extra vehicle was added to the Brown, Marshall order, originally for 24 vans. It was their official photograph of Van No. 7 which appeared in the Directors' Albums. Both series of vans were identical in construction, the most noticeable difference between the two manufacturers' products being the layout of the lettering: the first ampersand being in the same panel as the 'W R', thus giving a more balanced layout on the Gloucester vehicles. Gloucester also blocked the lettering to the right and below in black, although whether this was done especially for the works photograph or this was actually the finished livery in which the vans ran in service is not clear. The Gloucester vehicles also had tare weights painted on the body framing, rather than the bottom plank as evident on Brown, Marshall's photograph.

Stoves were provided in the Gloucester vans but not in Brown, Marshall's products, although it seems likely that this omission would have been remedied by the H&BR in due course. Vans from both builders had only four brake blocks apiece. Common dimensions from both builders' vans were the 10ft wheelbase and the bodies: 10ft long (discounting the verandahs), by 7ft 9in wide. These thirty vans were only of 8 tons weight; as early as November 1886 Stirling was proposing to uprate ten vans, presumably to 12 tons. In due course all except the first two vans were indeed uprated: Kirtley's specifications were clearly inadequate for a heavily-graded line relying on mineral traffic.

The Gloucester Carriage & Wagon Co. charged £157 for each of their vans, and it is likely that Brown, Marshall's vehicles cost a similar amount. Further purchases of vans were to Stirling's more modern specifications: 40 twelve ton vans had been added to stock by 1901, and by 1922 the total had risen to 112, including 45 twenty ton vans - a reflection of the H&BR's efforts to run heavier trains.

Meanwhile, Vans No. 1 (star of the Gloucester Carriage & Wagon Co's. photograph), and No. 2 had been designated as Ballast Brake Vans and No. 11 had become a Tool Van at Cudworth. Around May 1916, ten H&BR vans (including Kirtley No. 5, 12, 18 and 25), were hired by the South Eastern & Chatham Railway along with fourteen Stirling 0-6-0's, in order to cope with the vast increase in military traffic bound for France. The H&BR vans were boarded 'For use on S.E.& C.R. only', and were allocated to specific duties in order to release 20-ton SECR vans for other duties.

One H&BR van each worked on trains between Erith and Hither Green; Bricklayers Arms and Gravesend West; Paddock Wood and Ashford; Hither Green and Westerham; but in pairs between Herne Hill and Sevenoaks, and later between Bricklayers Arms to Caterham and return.

After 1923, the LNER allocated Nos.HB4801 to HB4908 to the surviving H&BR Brake Vans which meant that five vans had met their demise or been transferred out of main line service. The rest would have disappeared around the late 1940's, although one H&BR Brake Van survived at Langley Park Colliery near Durham City until possibly the mid-1960's.

Plate 18 **H&BR Cattle Wagon No. 490.** One of twenty built by Brown, Marshall & Co. Again reuse of existing designs by Kirtley from his LC&DR experience is very evident – the contemporary LC&DR wagons were almost identical in appearance.

ROLLING STOCK LIVERIES

To avoid repetition it has been considered better to deal with the colours and finishes of the rolling stock in one complete section.

The locomotives are shown in grey primer finish with various parts picked out in tones of grey; highly polished parts were white-washed over or smeared with grease in order to avoid highlight reflections. This was done because the available photographic chemicals were not pan-chromatic and so could not render true tonal qualities; red, a particularly intense colour, became indistinguishable from black in pre-1920's film; similarly, blues and greens became 'washed-out'. So once a locomotive had posed for its photograph, it was normally returned to the paint shop to receive its service finish.

In the case of the Kirtley H&BR locomotives, this was but a slight modification of that on the London, Chatham & Dover Railway. The H&BR engines were a deep glossy black, panelled with $1^1/2$in. slate grey bands edged both sides in Vermilion, with a slight gap between the lining and banding. Corners were incurved, and panels appeared on tender or bunker ends as well as cabsides and tanks as seen in the photographs. Footplate drop angles and splashers had thin grey edging with a single red line within. The smokebox, chimney, firebox backhead, coal space, footplate and all below it were in dull black Japan, but Vermilion was applied to bufferbeams, insides of engine frames and axles. Bufferbeams were also edged in black and carried the letters "N°" plus locomotive number in gold serifed characters some 7in. high countershaded left and below in black, on either side of the drawhook. This was kept well burnished along with buffer heads and shanks, coupling rods, safety valve levers, smokebox door hinges, handles and joint rims; also the handrails and knobs. All visible copper pipes and brass fittings such as the safety valve columns, whistle, lubricator 'pots', clack valves, joint ring between boiler and smokebox, cab spectacle frames and the raised parts of the cast brass builders and numberplates were kept well polished, the background of the plates being painted in black. Cab interiors were purple-brown edged black with a fine Vermilion line between both, and finally the whole engine above footplate level was finished in several coats of best Copal Varnish

Matthew Stirling introduced a few changes with his first designs in 1889, and these gradually spread throughout the fleet. The major change was to add Brunswick Green to the black in equal proportions, giving a black finish but with green highlights: a combination known as 'Invisible Green'. The broad grey lining bands became Ultramarine Blue; a yellow border appeared between the Vermilion and black edging on bufferbeams, the black ends of which had red borders with incurved corners. Cab interiors were changed to Indian Red with a fine yellow line added inside the Vermilion one; flared copings around tender tops now received blue borders outside a thin red line (Kirtley simply had a single Vermilion line applied around the upper edge). Single red lines were usually painted on steps, axle ends, wheel rims, frame edges, tender axlebox covers, top and bottom spring leaves and buckles and retained on footplate drop angles, from which the grey lines were omitted.

The monogram of the initials 'HB&WRJR' in gilt scroll letters edged in reddish-brown was replaced by block letters 'H & B R' in gold, shaded to the right in red blended to brown below, with white highlights and around 6in high excluding shading. No other changes in lining or livery occurred except as a result of larger boilers and new cabs being fitted to some of the tender engines as detailed in the relevant sections. Although the livery may seem to be drab, it should be borne in mind that the engines were polished until they assumed more of a vitreous rather than a metallic quality; it is on record that Stirling himself took a great interest in the turn-out of the engines for the Sheffield services, to the

Plate 19 **H&BR Goods Brake Van No. 7.** Built by Brown, Marshall & Co. these brake vans were 18ft long over body on a wheelbase of 10ft. Minor differences in lettering can be seen between the Brown, Marshall and Gloucester built example (see plate 20) as explained in the narrative. No. 7 also has a prominent oil lamp housing.

extent of donning white cotton gloves to feel down the backs of the spokes. If the Bosses gloves came out with dirt on them, woe betide the cleaners.

The carriage stock, as on the LC&DR, was largely in Varnished Teak with roofs and lamp vents painted in white lead. Lettering was in 3in block characters in gold, shaded to the right in Crimson blended to black below, with white highlights (Stirling changed the shading to blue in 1906). The monogram appeared on Third class carriages, the Composites being graced with the transferred armorial device of the company in full colour and some 13³/₄in diameter overall. The full title 'Hull, Barnsley and West Riding Junction Railway and Dock Company' was in small, gold block letters on the brown outer band, inside which was a gold quatrefoil surrounding the coats-of-arms of Hull and Barnsley; a gold wheel with silver wings above; and a gold anchor with two green dolphins intertwined, below. The background for Hull's shield was erroneously coloured white, changed to green by the 1890's and finally assumed the correct Azure Blue with the third style, from 1905. This version also carried the shorter version of the Company's title, and some modest gilt leaf work appeared at the base of the device.

Solebars and buffer beams were painted in imitation teak finish and varnished; buffer heads were polished steel, but the stocks and all other ironwork below the solebars and frames were finished in black Japan. The Mansell wheels were varnished or painted medium brown with white rims; destination boards and brackets were finished as for the solebars, with white lettering on the boards themselves.

The Horse Boxes and Carriage Trucks may well have been varnished originally, but latterly were painted light brown with black lining and ironwork, then varnished. The insides of the Carriage Trucks were dark grey. The Breakdown Train vehicles were painted brown, but became light blue under the LNER, and finally all-over black under BR.

Wagon stock was all initially in lead or dark slate grey (darker in hue than shown in the photographs, which suggests a photographic grey finish applied specially). White block unshaded numbers and letters were 6in tall; the load limit in 3in script, and the tare weight 2in high.

The brake vans were similar, with white roofs and ceilings and buff interiors. Letters and figures were in 6in block characters shaded black, the tare weights being in 3in white letters on the crib rails, or a larger script on the bottom plank. Cattle and covered van interiors were finished in stone colour, with dark grey floors.

After 1892 lettering became 'H & B R' only, in 6in block letters changed five years later to 17in high where possible. On low-side wagons the 6in high numbers appeared centrally on each side thus: 'H & (number) B R'. After 1905, the additional legend 'CONTINENTAL ROUTE VIA HULL' in 6in block characters appeared on the top planks of high-sided wagons and at a corresponding height on some vans.

Vacuum fitted vans were painted red-brown. Wagon tarpaulins were lettered 'H & B R' in large block letters and given white edged red cross stripes, and ropes with one white and two red strands.

Very few wagons were repainted in NER livery, but those surviving under the LNER appeared in dark grey with the initials 'N E' in 18in characters. Numbers remained the same, in 5in figures prefixed with 'HB' in 9in letters.

Even fewer H&BR goods wagons survived to be taken over by BR, and probably any which did were withdrawn without repainting, but those vehicles fortunate enough to be sold on into private service received their new owners' liveries - such as they were. For example, wagons which went to the Tyne Improvement Commission merely received a blue painted patch about midway up the left end of the body sides with the initials 'TIC' and the new number. The previous livery was simply allowed to peel away.

Under the Hull & Barnsley Stock Fund's ownership, restoration has involved the reapplication of appropriate H&BR. liveries; Van 2 being again resplendent in glossy Brown after years in BR Departmental Black and before that, LNER Blue.

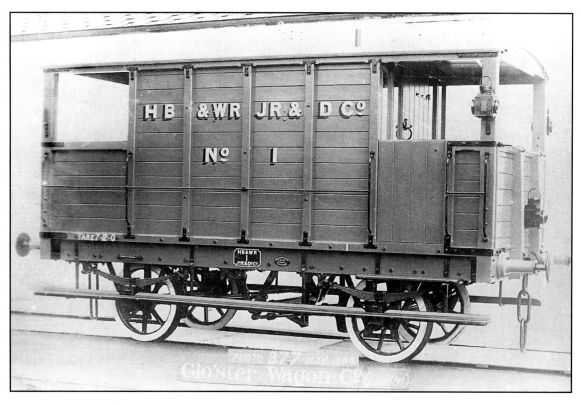

Plate 20 **H&BR Goods Brake Van No. 1.** The same design as Brake Van No. 7 seen in plate 19 but built by Gloucester Carriage & Wagon Co. and completed in May 1884. Whilst six vehicles were built by Gloucester C&W one was sold to the contractors, Lucus & Aird, so in consequence another one was added to Brown, Marshall's order.